T0312223

BINDING
EARTH
AND
HEAVEN

GARY SHEPHERD AND GORDON SHEPHERD

BINDING EARTH AND HEAVEN

PATRIARCHAL BLESSINGS
IN THE PROPHETIC DEVELOPMENT
OF EARLY MORMONISM

THE PENNSYLVANIA STATE UNIVERSITY PRESS
UNIVERSITY PARK, PENNSYLVANIA

Library of Congress Cataloging-in-Publication Data
Shepherd, Gary, 1943–
Binding earth and heaven : patriarchal blessings in the
prophetic development of early Mormonism /
Gary Shepherd and Gordon Shepherd.
p. cm.
Includes bibliographical references and index.
Summary: "Focuses on Mormonism as a case study of how
unpopular new religions may survive and even flourish in
spite of unrelenting opposition. Examines early patriarchal
blessings bestowed upon early converts to Mormonism
from 1834–1845, and their function as a commitment
mechanism for converts"—Provided by publisher.
ISBN 978-0-271-05633-3 (cloth : alk. paper)
ISBN 978-0-271-05634-0 (pbk. : alk. paper)
1. Patriarchal blessings (Mormon Church).
2. Church of Jesus Christ of Latter-day Saints—
History—19th century.
3. Mormon Church—History—19th century.
I. Shepherd, Gordon, 1943– .
II. Title.

BX8643.P36S54 2012
264'.09332013—dc23
2012020544

The Pennsylvania State University Press is a member of
the Association of American University Presses.

It is the policy of The Pennsylvania State University Press
to use acid-free paper. Publications on uncoated stock
satisfy the minimum requirements of American National
Standard for Information Sciences—Permanence of Paper
for Printed Library Material, ANSI Z39.48-1992.

To Lauren and Faye

CONTENTS

TABLES

PREFACE

In this book we explore several ways in which the unique Mormon theory and practice of issuing "patriarchal blessings" contributed to the early development of Mormonism as an ultimately successful new religious movement, in spite of widely held perceptions that the Mormons constituted a heretical religious and social menace. Mormon patriarchal blessings were an innovative adaptation of the Old Testament practice of fathers making quasi-legal pronouncements over the heads of their sons—a way of verbally conferring rights and promises, admonition and guidance, to heirs. They were introduced as a restored practice by Mormonism's founder, Joseph Smith, about three years after he formally incorporated his church in 1830. By 1835, Smith had greatly expanded the theological significance of these blessings and connected them to a divinely legitimated priesthood office: the office of church patriarch.[1] He also expanded the blessing recipient category to include all faithful members of the church, male and female. Thereafter, large numbers of Mormons living in proximity of the holder of this office avidly sought out a blessing from the ordained Patriarch. The theological and organizational complexities of this practice—and especially its contributions to strengthening and sustaining member faith and fealty, bolstering the continuity and development of Mormonism as a new religion—are elaborated in the chapters that follow.

We do not, however, propose in this book to write a detailed narrative of the institutional history of the office and duties of LDS Church Patriarchs in the full context of Mormon history. To an impressive degree, this has already been accomplished by Irene Bates and E. Gary Smith in their book *Lost Legacy: The Mormon Office of Presiding Patriarch*.[2] Nor do we intend to painstakingly document the gradual modification of the mode and thematic content of blessings issued to church members from the 1830s until the present day. We simply do not have the necessary documentary data for that purpose. Instead, our focus is on the first decade of the institution of patriarchal blessings, from 1834 to 1845, a concentrated and dramatic period of Mormon history that preceded the division of the Latter-day Saint community in Nauvoo, Illinois, and the embarkation in 1846 of Mormon pioneers—under the leadership of Brigham Young—to the Rocky Mountains of the American West.

We focus on this period for two reasons. First, we are primarily interested in the early, crucible years of new religions when they must either fail and expire or develop the organizational means and institutional authority for their continued survival. We believe and argue that the establishment of patriarchal blessings was an important element in the complex of revelatory and restorationist beliefs and practices that contributed to the LDS Church's survival. Second, we are fortunate to have access to a large recorded set of patriarchal blessings bestowed by the first three Mormon Presiding Patriarchs for the period 1834–45. These blessings constitute the essential primary data for our study and analysis. Other studies of the thematic content of LDS patriarchal blessings have been attempted, but few have systematically focused on blessings issued in the crucial years of early Mormon development.[3] Furthermore, the documentary sources for these blessings are haphazardly dispersed in widely varying time periods, making it difficult to ascertain how representative they are for showing how thematic blessing themes shifted over time.[4] Having said this, it is still possible for us to make some broad comparisons of early patriarchal blessings with those bestowed and cherished by Mormons today, which we summarize in the final chapter of this book.

We would like to make one final observation about the approach we take in this book as academic sociologists. Social science teaches that the institutions of any society, including religious institutions, are formed and changed through meaningful human interaction. Alternatively, we may simply say that all human institutions are socially constructed.[5] The province of social science is the naturalistic analysis of how the organization and patterns of human life are socially negotiated and agreed upon, the problems that human communities confront in this process (including the modification and fracturing of agreements), and the consequences that ensue for both individuals and group culture.

If there be extra-human agency or supernatural powers ultimately involved in the human construction of history and society, it is not, strictly speaking, the province of social science to judge and determine their ontological authenticity. More specifically, it is not the province of social science to validate or invalidate the ultimate truth claims of religious faith. For this we must turn to metaphysics or theology and to a consideration of the various religious epistemologies employed by seekers of transcendent meaning. While methodologically agnostic with respect to transcendent causes and ultimate meanings, social science analysis can nonetheless contribute significantly to our understanding of the human aspects of religious institutions and religious ways of life.

We are indebted to Michael Marquardt's superior scholarship in assembling the large collection of Smith patriarchal blessings, which constitutes the basis of our empirical analysis for this book, and for his suggestion to us that we carry out this analysis in the first place. We are grateful to Michael Quinn for an early, helpful critique of a portion of what emerged as our book; to Jan Shipps for early encouragement to pursue this project and subsequent endorsement of it; to Armand Mauss for his suggestions and strong support of our manuscript when it was undergoing critical review; and to Lavina Fielding Anderson for sharing advanced versions of her own parallel patriarchal blessing research accompanied by valuable insights and recommendations concerning ours. We also are grateful for the various contributions of Gordon's three daughters: Natalie arduously coded the blessing contents, Lynne posed and photographed the image on our book's cover, and Pam lent her layout expertise. Finally, we acknowledge and applaud the professional competence of The Pennsylvania State University Press. In particular, Kendra Boileau displayed assiduous editorial guidance and maintained her faith in our project even when we briefly lost ours. Laura Reed-Morrisson performed superb plastic surgery on the text and helped us craft a much cleaner final version. Jennifer Norton was open to suggestions and then worked with Jason Harvey to design the striking book cover, and Brian Beer was flexible and efficient in generating publicity. Any errors of fact or interpretation in the book are, of course, ours.

INTRODUCTION

With a current official membership of more than 14,000,000 worldwide, the Church of Jesus Christ of Latter-day Saints (or LDS Church) is one of the fastest-growing religious denominations in the United States as well as in numerous other countries.[1] Headquartered in Salt Lake City, Utah, the capital city of a staunchly Republican state, the LDS Church is widely known for its advocacy of wholesome lifestyles, traditional gender roles, and conservative family values. Two Mormon former state governors—Mitt Romney (Massachusetts) and John Huntsman (Utah)—vied as Republican Party candidates for President of the United States in 2011, with Romney emerging by the spring of 2012 as the presumptive Republican nominee (after an earlier failed attempt in 2008).[2]

A mere century and a quarter ago, however, on the floor of the U.S. House of Representatives, Ezra B. Taylor of Ohio denounced the "Mormon menace" in unequivocal language:

> An earnest, resolute, and even fanatical people have taken possession of one of the large Territories of the Union, seized upon the public domain, organized and established a church which absorbs as well as controls the state . . . and made it not an empire in an empire, but the empire itself . . . This people and this church defy the moral sense of the civilized world and are of necessity antagonistic to the principles and institution of the Republic. . . . They defy such laws as thwart their needs and interests, and the time has arrived when it must be decided whether they rule or obey.[3]

The 1887 deliberations of the Edmunds-Tucker Bill—punitive anti-polygamy legislation, which Congressman Taylor was advocating—signaled the culmination of several decades of intense political struggle between the United States government and the Utah LDS Church. Beginning in the early 1830s, the "Mormons" had undergone years of intense opposition in the Midwestern states of Ohio, Missouri, and Illinois; thirteen years prior to the outbreak of the U.S. Civil War they had fled to the Rocky Mountains in search of religious refuge. Following a period of relative tranquility and insular theocracy in the Utah Territory, an expeditionary force of the United States Army was dispatched in 1857 to depose Brigham Young as territorial governor and reinforce federal executive and judicial authority among the supposedly rebellious Mormons.

By the late nineteenth century, Mormonism was universally despised and had become the target of an unprecedented national campaign to extirpate polygamy and the theocratic institutions of the LDS Church. In the American South, especially, the means employed against the "Mormon menace" included not only legislation and religion but also vigilante violence directed against Mormon missionaries who dared preach their heretical faith in Southern states. In his study of second-generation Mormonism's relationship to postbellum America, Patrick Mason makes the case that anti-Mormonism became an important cultural mechanism for reconciling the North and South following the Civil War by uniting nominally decent, God-fearing citizens in both regions of the country against what was increasingly portrayed by politicians, clergymen, and the mass media as a malignant religious tumor on the body of Christian America.[4] It is doubtful that the history of any other American religion surpasses the sustained conflict and opposition, often involving violence or the threat of violence, which the Latter-day Saints had to overcome before firmly establishing the legitimacy of their religious faith.

THE PROBLEM OF COMMITMENT IN HERETICAL NEW RELIGIONS

In the face of fierce opposition by established religious traditions and secular authorities—opposition that often includes extralegal violence as well as relentless legal prosecutions—we may ask, How do heretical new religions sustain their resilience and the resolute commitment of their members? By "heretical," of course, we do not mean intrinsically wrong or wicked. We simply mean doctrines and corresponding practices that are at variance with the authority of established orthodoxies.[5] It will not do to simply say that such groups consist of deluded fanatics in the thrall of egomaniacal leaders. This explains very little.[6] Embattled new religions that endure, and even flourish over time, must effectively appeal to the religious aspirations of some segment of what Rodney Stark and William Bainbridge call a "religious economy."[7] An active religious economy can exist when religious freedom, and therefore religious choice, is countenanced by the political institutions of the state. For a new religion to attract and then retain converts in a religious economy, it must, in the first instance, have market appeal—it must appeal to religious consumers who are already predisposed to certain core values and beliefs but are dissatisfied with what currently is offered by established religions. In the second instance, assuming market appeal to some segment of a religious economy, we must ask: Exactly what is it that new religions actually *do* to preserve, and even strengthen, the faith and loyalty of their converted members when faced with concerted opposition to the promulgation of their putatively heretical beliefs and practices? Those socially fostered attitudes, practices, and rituals that serve to reinforce members' compliance with group requirements in pursuit of group goals may be called "commitment mechanisms." Effective commitment mechanisms are an essential aspect of the institutional structure of any enduring organization or community.[8] It is this second concern with convert commitment that is our primary focus in this book.

THE CASE OF MORMONISM

Taking early Mormonism as a strategic case study,[9] we address in this book the question of how embattled new religions may survive and even flourish by focusing on one particular complex of LDS beliefs, rituals, and practices—the institution of patriarchal blessings—that emerged as an important compensatory commitment mechanism in the nineteenth-century Mormon restoration movement. Patriarchal blessings were neither the only nor single most important commitment mechanism operating in early Mormon development—far from it. In a prior study, we identified a broad range of different activities, rules, beliefs, and organizational characteristics that elicited Mormon faith and loyalty in the face of opposition, hardship, and doubt.[10] But because both the content and process of obtaining patriarchal blessings combine and emphasize several key elements of Mormon theology—such as revelation and prophetic guidance, priesthood authority, the millennial end times, building the Kingdom of God on earth, lineal continuity with the ancient Israelites as God's covenant people, eternal salvation through sacrificial obedience, and other related themes—we believe that they were a particularly potent vehicle for bolstering early Mormon faithfulness. At the same time, patriarchal blessings were also a means of solidifying and reinforcing convert understanding of unique Mormon tenets by articulating these in powerful, personalized, prophetic language for recipients of those blessings.

As noted above, securing faith and loyalty from followers must, of course, be preceded by their initial attraction to a group. The rise and spread of nineteenth-century Mormonism demonstrates a necessary correspondence between the relative success of a new religion and its market appeal to some segment of a religious economy. Those individuals to whom early Mormonism most appealed were Bible-reading Christians who were seeking a restoration of New Testament visionary religion; they were already primed to accept and be guided by prophetic pronouncements contained in revelations and blessings as God's Word to the contemporary world.[11] While the origins of most prophetic new religions like Mormonism naturally draw attention to the character and claims of their charismatic founders, the actual inception, construction, and subsequent development of enduring new religions also need to be understood as the collective result of like-minded collaborators and devoted disciples in interaction with outsiders and well-entrenched establishment institutions.

It is worth noting that the emergence and development of a new religion, as it takes on organizational form, is simultaneously a unifying and divisive phenomenon. The polarizing character of religious movements is especially true of religions like Mormonism that proclaim the charismatic authority of divine revelation and prophetic guidance in connection with their origins and subsequent development. Many people (especially religious officials and the clergy) are offended by a new religion's perceived heretical challenge to the doctrines and practices of established religious traditions. They may feel compelled to oppose or even engage in active suppression of what they believe to be dangerous religious falsehoods. In contrast, other people—those who constitute the market for the appeals of a new religion—become convinced that they have found precisely what they were looking for. While most converts entertain occasional doubts, the truly committed not only articulate verbal justifications for their religious commitments but also are willing to make significant personal sacrifices in defense of their new faith.[12]

Over time, many converts to new religions remain steadfast or even increase their devotion, while others eventually become disillusioned and withdraw their commitments. Of those converts who become disillusioned, a certain number—typically a statistical minority—become "apostates." That is, as former group members, they become actively engaged in opposing or attempting to suppress the new faith they once embraced.[13] All of these convert categories and commitment phases are dramatically demonstrated in the early years of Mormon history. In this book, however, we are primarily concerned with those early converts who remained sufficiently committed to their faith and the organizational means employed for strengthening it, thereby sustaining the continuity and development of Mormonism as a new religion.

RELIGIOUS POLARIZATION AND THE STRONG CHARISMA OF ORACULAR PROPHECY

Weberian scholar Edward Shils argues that most people, most of the time, value order over uncertainty, and that those individuals who are able to dispel human confusion and uncertainty creatively, through their art, science, philosophy, or leadership in economic, political, military, or religious affairs, are accorded the highest respect by their peers: "Whatever embodies, expresses, or symbolizes the essence of an ordered cosmos or any significant sector thereof awakens the disposition of awe and reverence, the charismatic disposition."[14] According to Shils, the "charismatic disposition"—the propensity to attribute extraordinary (or even supernatural) gifts and authority to innovators and supremely confident leaders—is intrinsic to the human condition in all societies and historical epochs.

It is in the context of religious issues concerning ultimate value and meaning, especially in times of uncertainty, stress, and upsetting social changes, that "charisma" is often attributed to the founders of new faiths that arise to challenge the cosmological and moral foundations of precursor faiths. Prototypical prophets, such as Moses, Jesus, and Muhammad, issue authority claims that stand outside the normative structures of tradition or law and, in fact, typically call into question the legitimacy of existing institutional authority. The words and moral vision of the prophet are attributed to a transcendent source and, through claims of divine guidance, command compliance in the name of God as being wholly superior to any worldly authority or human power. All would-be prophets do not, of course, succeed in winning converts to their transcendent claims. The only empirical test of prophetic charismatic authority is whether a sufficient number of followers willingly acknowledge the prophet's claims and render loyal obedience to his or her moral mandates in order to sustain a new religious community.[15]

The claim of transcendent authority and supernatural power in support of new or alternative doctrines and practices typically is much stronger for religious converts than claims made on mere grounds of reason or any form of human authority. In particular, those prophetic religions that attract followers on the basis of what we will call *oracular* prophecy are most likely to be polarizing religions. Oracles are considered to be spiritual intermediaries (or prophets, in the Islamic and Judeo-Christian traditions) through whom ultimate truths are directly transmitted. These truths are thought by believers to transcend the range of ordinary human knowledge or understanding. As a form of communication, oracular prophecy is typically declarative and highly personalized; by announcing a divine message, it aims to have a stimulating and motivational effect on people's thoughts and actions.

More specifically, oracular prophecies consist of revelatory pronouncements formulated as the literal voice of God or other divine entities, channeled through selected prophetic oracles, for instructing, admonishing, and rewarding human actors in exchange for their obedience. Obedience in this context, of course, means compliance with what are construed as God's laws, commandments, and divine principles that typically set adherents apart from nonbelievers. The Hebrew Decalogue popularly attributed to Moses's Mount Sinai theophany and Muhammad's dictation of the Holy Qur'an are prime examples of oracular prophecy; they are echoed in Joseph Smith's religious narrative as prophet and founder of nineteenth-century Mormonism. When formalized in writing and officially certified by the recognized authorities of a particular religious tradition, such pronouncements attain the status of holy writ or scripture for guiding and judging adherents of the faith.

Oracular prophecy can be contrasted with what we will call *inspirational* prophecy. Like oracular prophecy, inspirational prophecy may also be canonized in scripture, but its style of communication is typically expository and less personal. It too aims to stimulate and inspire followers to action in God's name but claims only God's sanction and approval. Inspirational prophecy is less radical than oracular prophecy, less strong and demanding; it does not profess to dictate God's words, verbatim, to the people. For example, *ex cathedra* pronouncements contained in papal encyclicals issued by the Catholic Church are considered by Catholics to be revelations of God's will to his vicar on earth, but they are scarcely expressed in the language of oracular prophecy. In contrast to what might be called the "strong charisma" of oracular prophecy, the milder charisma of inspirational prophecy tends to be less polarizing. One common historical pattern among prophetic religions that, like Mormonism, manage to survive the vicissitudes of their origins and become established denominations in the religious economy is that they move from their oracular origins to increasing reliance on less radical forms of inspirational prophecy as their chief mode of guidance.[16]

The strong charisma of oracular prophecy is fundamentally supported by what Garry Wills calls "ultra-supernaturalism."[17] We employ this term to highlight the beliefs of actors in the religious economy who insist on the ever-present reality of spirit entities that direct human destiny. Prior to the advent of eighteenth-century Enlightenment scholarship and science, such a distinction would seem largely superfluous in Western culture. Both Catholic and Protestant societies were once dominated by such beliefs. Three hundred years ago, there was virtual consensus on the proximate reality of an active spirit world—regardless of the governing religion—that sustained a miraculous rather than a naturalistic worldview. It is only from the vantage point of later, more skeptical centuries, in which Christian belief systems have gradually been tempered and much modified in response to scientific naturalism, that adding the prefix "ultra" to "supernatural" gives us a useful term for retrospectively describing the most emphatic kinds of supernatural beliefs in a designated religious economy. The cultural relationship between the plausibility of oracular claims and ultra-supernaturalism can be stated simply: The plausibility of oracular prophecy, in which spirit entities verbally communicate with human oracles, is greatly enhanced for people living in cultural environments where ultra-supernatural beliefs prevail. Conversely, the weaker the prevalence of ultra-supernaturalism in a designated cultural environment, the less plausible oracular claims are for a larger number of people.[18]

Ultra-supernatural beliefs characterize religious cultures that posit the existence of supernatural entities and a spirit world transcending mundane human existence. They also emphasize the permeability of the boundary separating the spirit world from the natural world. In the ultra-supernatural worldview, various spirit entities are believed to routinely breach the veil between heaven and earth, appearing before human actors in dramatic displays of their superhuman powers. At the same time, human reports of being transported in time and space to experience contact with and receive verbal instruction or empowerment from transcendent entities are given reverential credence by believers. Ultra-supernatural beliefs serve to explain virtually every aspect of daily life and human history as the result of supernatural intervention in human affairs. In the monotheistic faith traditions of ancient Judaism, Christianity, and Islam, supernatural intervention was portrayed as an integral element in the struggle between good and evil—literalized in ultra-supernatural beliefs as a ferocious spiritual clash between the evil forces of the Devil and the godly forces of Heaven. Through the lens of ultra-supernatural belief, human conflicts are interpreted as the dramatic unfolding of this cosmic clash: anthropomorphized specific spirit entities, both good and evil, relentlessly labor to achieve their conflicting ends by deploying miraculous powers and recruiting human agents into the struggle.

Members of new religions founded in oracular prophecy are nourished by cultures that sustain an ultra-supernatural world view. They typically believe that they have been granted privileged possession of ultimate truth and the efficacious (often esoteric) means for validating it through various forms of studious inquiry, prayer, meditation, ritual, abstinence, self-mortification, substance ingestion, hypnotic trance states, and so on. All of the latter, with the exception of substance ingestion and hypnotic states, are recommended by Latter-day Saints as means of validating the exclusive truth claims of their religion. Patriarchal blessings in particular may be understood as a ritual practice that Mormons believe constitutes a spiritual medium for revealing God's personalized intentions in the lives of blessing recipients, both individually and collectively as God's covenant people.

Increasing secularism and the rationalizing forces of modernity notwithstanding, ultra-supernaturalism has been a major and persistent cultural element in American history. It characterized the religious worldview of the New England Puritans (cultural ancestors of many of Mormonism's early leaders, including Joseph Smith and his successor, Brigham Young) and was an essential ingredient in the first and second "Great Awakenings" that fueled the rise of American evangelical Christianity in the nineteenth century.[19] Ultra-supernaturalism was an especially prevalent part of the cultural milieu of western New York state, where Joseph Smith grew to young manhood.[20] Today, similar ultra-supernatural beliefs continue to be strongly emphasized by many contemporary evangelical Christians and Pentecostals.[21] Our exposition of the themes of early Mormon patriarchal blessings will highlight the salience of ultra-supernatural beliefs shared by Mormonism's founding generation of leaders and followers.

The earliest version of Mormonism in America in the 1830s appealed to denominationally disaffected Christians (like Joseph Smith's father, Joseph Smith Sr.) who nonetheless professed ultra-supernatural beliefs and longed for the prophetic authority and spiritual gifts of New Testament Christianity.[22] As a new religious movement, Mormonism was unequivocally oracular in its mode of development and functioning during the brilliantly implausible career of its founder, Joseph Smith Jr. The prophet Joseph Smith exercised the strong charisma of oracular prophecy to build the doctrinal foundation of his followers' faith while providing decisive organizational leadership.

This is not to say that Smith's charismatic leadership was uncontested or produced only unity, not division. To the contrary, by enacting the role of God's chosen oracle for ushering in what his followers believed was the restoration of the true church of Jesus Christ in the last days of human history, Joseph Smith attracted intense repudiation and abhorrence, and intense devotion and admiration, in equal measure. Even within the Mormon community, the prophet was a polarizing figure. His oracular pronouncements were not confined to a single, initial, comprehensive statement of God's will. Rather, they continued and were increasingly elaborate as he expanded the scope of his theological and organizational ideas over the course of a fourteen-year prophetic career. While many followers thrilled in the belief that a modern-day prophet was guiding them with constant updates from God and welcomed the innovations that resulted, more than a few early converts to the Book of Mormon soon became agitated and disaffected by the newly revealed doctrinal and policy edicts— some of them seemingly contradictory—that issued from Smith's fertile mind.[23] A number of his erstwhile lieutenants and early counselors turned on him, some seeking to take his life (antagonistic episodes of this type are highlighted in chapter 2). Nevertheless, the cohesiveness and proliferation of early Mormonism would be virtually inconceivable without the strong oracular religious foundations laid by Joseph Smith.

At the same time, early Mormonism's rapid spread did not depend solely on oracular prophecy. Among a variety of additional factors,[24] it also resulted from the organizational authority given to other individuals among his followers to speak and act in the name of God—to pronounce, in the capacity of various lay priesthood offices to which a number of faithful Mormon men were ordained, what they believed was revelation from God for the instruction, admonition, guidance, and encouragement of Mormon converts. The earliest investigators and new converts to the religion commonly turned directly to Joseph Smith to seek personal answers from the prophet in resolving their questions. Indeed, a number of his first recorded revelations were precisely responses to queries of this sort.[25] However, delegation of authority to provide spiritual and practical guidance quickly became mandatory as convert numbers swelled and centers of Mormon activity dispersed over greater distances. Empowering other men with priesthood authority to speak in God's name and perform miraculous deeds for individual or local purposes was a significant element in early Mormonism's democratic appeal.

Chief among these additionally empowered oracles were the patriarchs of the church, who, through their "restored *sealing* authority," vouchsafed blessings to the people redeemable both on earth and in heaven.[26] (In Mormon parlance, to "seal" a blessing or relationship through priesthood authority signifies making a promised result legitimate and permanent, both in this life and in the life to come.) Patriarchal blessings were a highly important element in a constellation of emerging LDS practices for strengthening converts' ultra-supernatural faith, reinforcing their doctrinal understanding of what outsiders viewed as a Christian heresy,[27] and infusing them with a sense of their transcendent destiny, as God's chosen people, to restore what they believed was the true church and gospel of Jesus Christ in the last days of human time. In this book, we investigate the commitment and doctrinal exposition functions of those blessings in the lives of early LDS converts.

OVERVIEW OF THE BOOK

In chapter 1, we amplify our discussion of the supernatural valence of oracular prophecy in generating religious commitment and the charismatic appeal of early Mormonism to nineteenth-century restorationists. To provide essential historical context for understanding many of the doctrinal themes expressed in patriarchal blessings, in chapter 2 we narrate some of the chief episodes of early Mormon history, especially those that demonstrate the simultaneous social consequences of unity and conflict in oracular religious movements. In chapter 3 we focus on the origins of the office and calling of the patriarch and discuss the communal ritual characteristics of early patriarchal blessings and their distinctive role in reinforcing the religious commitment of LDS converts. Chapter 4 describes the available documentary sources of early Mormon patriarchal blessings, the value and limitations of using such documents to infer historical outcomes, and our methodology for drawing a sample of blessings and performing a systematic content analysis on them. Chapters 5 and 6 report the statistical thematic findings of our content analysis. In chapter 5, the twenty most common patriarchal blessing themes pronounced in the first decade of Mormon history are identified and analyzed as prophetic contributions to the promulgation of core LDS beliefs in a manner that strongly reinforced members' personal faith in those beliefs. Chapter 6 further advances our theme analysis by spotlighting gender as an important blessing variable. Our analysis of gender differences in early patriarchal blessings shows that, while reflecting nineteenth-century gender norms concerning male authority, blessings were relatively egalitarian in their thematic contents. Thus we are led to the primary conclusion that the patriarchal blessings for both Mormon men and women served to unite their commitments to the religious cause of the Latter-day Saint restoration. Finally, in chapter 7 we reflect on the changed character and relative decline in the institutional salience of contemporary LDS patriarchal blessings in comparison to the historical ascendance of other Mormon commitment mechanisms, especially those involved in LDS temple worship and the institution of general conference.

THE COMMITMENT AND DOCTRINAL FUNCTIONS OF EARLY MORMON PATRIARCHAL BLESSINGS

The study of early patriarchal blessings and their religious functions for converts to the Mormon restoration in the 1834–1845 period carries us historically to the great breach among Joseph Smith's followers—occasioned at the time of his death—and their subsequent division into contending doctrinal camps. Two principal denominational entities emerged from that division.

UTAH-BASED MORMONS AND THE COMMUNITY OF CHRIST

"Mormon," "Mormons," and "Mormonism" are, of course, popular nickname variants used in reference to the doctrines and members of the Church of Jesus Christ of Latter-day Saints (or LDS Church). To complicate matters further, early Mormonism generated numerous schisms following the assassination of its prophet-founder, Joseph Smith Jr., in June 1844.[1] In 1860 a number of these factional groups in the Midwestern states of Ohio, Illinois, Missouri, Iowa, and Michigan coalesced and were united under the leadership of Joseph Smith III, Joseph Smith Jr.'s oldest son, to form the Reorganized Church of Jesus Christ of Latter Day Saints (or RLDS Church).[2] From the outset of its organizational life, the RLDS Church attempted to assert an institutional identity separate from the much larger and better-known LDS community headquartered in Salt Lake City. Theologically, the RLDS Church distanced itself from the temple doctrines and ceremonies that emerged in Nauvoo, Illinois, prior to

Smith's assassination and were exported to the Utah territory under the leadership of Brigham Young and the Quorum of the Twelve Apostles. The RLDS Church emphatically renounced the doctrine of plural marriage and the practice of polygamy. On less portentous questions (but of symbolic significance in maintaining its distinctiveness), the RLDS Church dropped the hyphen in "Latter-day," capitalized "Day," and repudiated both the nickname of "Mormon" and the religious faith designation of "Mormonism."

Over time (especially since the latter half of the twentieth century), RLDS authorities have gradually reformulated the mission and identity of their community of believers. Rather than contesting the authority claims of the Utah-centered LDS Church, they have worked to identify the more universal aspects of their restoration beliefs that are congenial to other Christian faith traditions.[3] Thus, for example, in correspondence with the large-scale redefinition of gender roles taking place in the larger society and in liberal Protestant denominations, the RLDS Church announced in 1984 that women could be ordained to the RLDS priesthood (producing widespread support from many of its members but also substantial dissent and schism).[4] That same year, RLDS authorities also announced plans to construct a temple in Independence, Missouri (completed in 1994), that would be open to the public and dedicated to promoting a Christ-centered theology of peace and justice. This contrasts sharply with the operation of scores of LDS temples worldwide that serve as religious edifices for the performance of exclusive temple ceremonies that reinforce LDS religious commitments, thereby accentuating differences between Latter-day Saints and non–Latter-day Saints (a theme that we will elaborate in succeeding chapters).[5]

Moving even further away from the original LDS identity, Wallace B. Smith retired as president of the RLDS Church in 1996 and was succeeded by W. Grant McMurray—the first non-Smith family member to preside over the RLDS Church in its 150-year history. Lineal male descent from the prophet Joseph is no longer considered a prerequisite for ascending to the office of president in the RLDS Church.[6] Most significantly, in 2001 the RLDS Church shed its LDS designation altogether and renamed itself the Community of Christ.[7] Currently the Community of Christ is pursuing official recognition by the National Council of Churches in conformity with the Council's doctrinal views on what constitutes a Christian religion. In contrast, because of its steadfast commitment to the veracity of Joseph Smith's prophetic claims, doctrinal innovations, and the Book of Mormon as an authentic scripture on par with the Bible, the Utah-headquartered LDS Church is not regarded by the National Council of Churches as a Christian denomination. (On their part, LDS authorities do not appear in the least concerned to gain the Council's approbation.)

At the same time, both the LDS Church and the Community of Christ continue to implement the practice of bestowing patriarchal blessings on their members today. We will briefly summarize current patriarchal blessing practices in the LDS and Community of Christ faith traditions in later chapters. Our main focus throughout the book, however, is the origin and early practice of LDS patriarchal blessings. In our discussion and analysis of these early blessings we find it convenient to employ the term "Mormon" and various LDS designations interchangeably. And since our primary focus is on early Mormonism, we will employ the hyphenated variation of Latter-day Saints in reference to the founding generation of Mormon converts who received patriarchal blessings from 1834 to 1845.

Quickly congealing organizationally into what early Mormon converts first identified as the Church of Christ in 1830 (soon renamed the Church of the Latter Day Saints and eventually the Church of Jesus Christ of Latter-day Saints),[8] today's Latter-day Saint and Community of Christ churches began as a prophet-centered new religion that forged its institutional foundations on the American frontier in the decades prior to the Civil War. Frederick Jackson Turner's now controversial but hugely influential thesis regarding the role of the shifting frontier in the historical formation of distinctly American attitudes and values—including individualism, distrust of national authority, intolerance of hierarchy (especially aristocratic hierarchies of inherited privilege), and self-righteous resort to violence as a means for defending or advancing one's material and political interests—must certainly be considered when assessing early Mormon history.[9] As a new religious movement forming on America's frontiers in the Ohio Western Reserve, Missouri, and Illinois at a time when they were border states to the Indian Territories, and ultimately in the mountainous deserts of the Utah Territory, nineteenth-century Mormonism was fundamentally shaped by its frontier experiences. These experiences were especially affected by violent conflict with other frontier Americans who felt repelled and threatened by Mormonism's most distinctive religious teachings, clannish insularity, and political solidarity. Indeed, according to Jan Shipps, the history of nineteenth-century Mormon conflict with other

Americans can only be adequately understood by recognizing the densely intertwined opposition of both religious and secular forces to oracular LDS doctrinal claims and theocratic political aspirations.[10] It was, Shipps concludes, this potent combination of both religious and secular antagonism that branded the Latter-day Saints as not merely being different from other Christian denominations in the American religious economy, but as decidedly threatening and alien, or "other," therefore posing a consensual target of attack.

For two generations following their colonization of the Great Basin region of the Rocky Mountains, Utah Mormons—who continued to insist that their religion was revealed by God and guided by contemporary prophets—faced unrelenting legal and extralegal opposition. The primary concern of Utah Mormons was not intramural authority and doctrinal disputes within the Latter-day restoration movement itself. Rather, their concern was to sustain and defend their mountain theocracy from external opposition, including (and especially) the federal government's ultimately successful efforts to assert secular political authority and abolish the practice of polygamy. This was accomplished only after a protracted struggle, highlighted by the imposition and continuing threat of military force and two decades of increasingly draconian legal measures that legitimated the confiscation of church property and the suspension of polygamists' civil rights through passage of the Edmunds-Tucker Bill in 1887.[11]

Forced to relinquish theocratic involvement in politics and the practice of plural marriage, the Utah Latter-day Saints gradually moved in the direction of support for and integration into the political economy of American society. Their subsequent history has been one of sustained and eventually prolific growth in both the American and global religious economies of the twentieth and twenty-first centuries.[12] This growth can be attributed to a massive and highly organized missionary effort whose message of prophetic guidance, family values, and lay religious activity resonates with people who are seeking institutional authority, moral certitude, a strong sense of community identification, and active involvement in what they believe is a transcendent cause.[13] As a highly successful missionary religion, one of the most distinctive and important group commitment mechanisms employed historically by the LDS Church for reinforcing the faith of members and new converts was and (though now less salient) continues to be the institution of patriarchal blessings.

GROUP COMMITMENT MECHANISMS AND THE SUPERNATURAL
VALENCE OF ORACULAR PROPHECY

Commitment mechanisms are those social practices (including rituals) that unite people while reinforcing shared beliefs and values that justify the expenditure of their resources in compliance with group requirements in the pursuit of group goals. Shared commitments are, of course, precisely what make human communities strong and resilient. To the degree that shared commitments weaken, communities lose their unity and resilience.[14] Generating and maintaining group commitment is particularly crucial for the survival of emergent radical groups, including new religions, which both challenge and are challenged by dominant, well-established groups. Based on a combination of prescriptive and proscriptive rules, commitment practices in most groups—especially in religious communities—typically involve group-sanctioned forms of self-denial, such as dietary restrictions, austerity norms, and sexual abstinence (or, conversely, in many new religions, development of unconventional sexual, marital, and family relationships that shift individuals' priority commitments from monogamous units to the larger community).

Community commitment is often also enhanced by constructing both physical and psychic boundaries: group members withdraw or separate themselves from routine contact with outsiders. Boundaries are maintained by emphasizing in-group self-sufficiency and upholding distinctive customs, speech patterns, modes of dress, or any other social markers and lifestyle requirements that set group members apart from people outside their community. Simultaneously, a distinctive way of life is strengthened by frequent in-group contacts through regularly scheduled meetings, community work projects, sharing of material resources, and other normative activities that routinely require the active cooperation of group members, generating a shared sense of mutual purpose and identification. To a greater or lesser degree, all of these commitment practices are plainly observable in the formation and strengthening of Mormon communities, both historically and at the present time.

Finally—through ritual, song, prayer, the symbolization of transcendent authority, and the exposition of core beliefs and aspirations—religious worship services in particular arouse strong emotional associations, reinforce people's shared convictions, justify their often sacrificial commitments to the community, and reassure them of ultimate compensation. During the early time period we are concerned with in this book, many patriarchal blessings were pronounced in group settings—specifically designated as "blessing meetings"—accompanied by prayers, hymn singing, and other symbolic accoutrements of collective worship. In this context, then, LDS patriarchal blessings can be understood as a particular type of religious ritual activity that functioned to strengthen individuals' faith and religious identities while simultaneously producing shared commitment to the religious community.

In chapter 3 and the concluding chapter of this book we discuss further the specific ritual characteristics of patriarchal blessings that make them a highly significant Mormon commitment mechanism. Here, however, we simply emphasize that the group consequence of sustaining and strengthening shared commitments may not always be the principal or even intended purpose of a particular ritual practice when it is originally instituted. For example, we may ask, What was the intended purpose of patriarchal blessings when they were instituted among the Latter-day Saints in 1834? The ecclesiastical innovation of the office of the patriarch and the patriarch's priesthood authority to bless the people was justified as part of the latter-day restoration, with particular reference to the Hebraic foundations of primitive Christianity. The purpose of the office and calling of the patriarch, instituted by Joseph Smith, was therefore understood by Mormon believers to be part of God's plan of redemption and salvation for the remnants of Israel as a new covenant people in the latter days of human history.[15]

As an understandable human motive, Richard Bushman also has suggested that Joseph Smith may have been influenced, out of affection and loyalty to his father, to create a serviceable position in which Joseph Sr. might restore his sense of self-worth, after an adult life of considerable failure, and be honored by the Latter-day Saint community.[16] Personal motives and theological beliefs aside, however, it does not matter whether the group commitment consequences of patriarchal blessings were initially intended by Joseph Smith or subsequently perceived and deliberately promoted by other Latter-day Saint leaders. Regardless of human actors' original intentions, if the latent consequences of a designated ritual or practice serve to reinforce shared commitments in compliance with group requirements and goals, then, *ipso facto,* that ritual or practice may be regarded and understood as a commitment mechanism.[17]

The most systematic and insightful analysis of commitment mechanisms in erstwhile utopian communities, whether religious or secular, arguably remains Rosabeth Kanter's *Commitment and Community.*[18] In

Kanter's study, communities most likely to be successful at retaining their members' affiliation, generating group solidarity, and exercising normative control over adherents' beliefs and practices are groups that strike the right balance between community demands and community rewards. Community demands of personal sacrifice must be adequately compensated by the anticipated rewards of material and spiritual investment returns. Community demands for renunciation of dependency on outsiders must be offset by mutual caring and communion with like-minded others. Finally, community demands for self-mortification in submission to the authority of the group must be validated by the cognitive-emotional transcendence of belief in ultimate meanings and purpose. In enduring new religions, both community demands and compensatory community rewards are typically instituted in a wide variety of social practices and rituals that vary in their particulars from one religious group or community to another. A thorough application of Kanter's theoretical analysis of commitment mechanisms to the institutional success of the LDS Church, both as a new religion in the nineteenth century and a major competitor in the world religious economy of the twenty-first century, constitutes a valuable approach for understanding Mormonism's historical sustainability and growth.

We of course do not argue that the LDS institution of patriarchal blessings was the only group commitment mechanism that preserved Mormonism as a new religious movement. Elsewhere we have, in fact, identified and discussed the relative salience of many of the interrelated commitment mechanisms that have been employed throughout the institutional history of the LDS Church.[19] Here, however, we contend that the doctrinal and commitment functions of patriarchal blessings in particular have not been adequately studied or appreciated. In our view, patriarchal blessings emerged in early Mormonism as a distinctive and important ritual practice for strengthening converts' faith, reinforcing their doctrinal understanding of what outsiders viewed as a Christian heresy, and infusing them with a sense of their transcendent destiny as God's chosen people for restoring what they believed was the true church and gospel of Jesus Christ in the last days. As part of the doctrinal foundation of the Mormon restoration, Latter-day Saints believed that the church patriarch, through the restored priesthood of his office, was both authorized and inspired to speak God's will in blessing the people. Thus, patriarchal blessings bestowed on individual church members were also considered to be a form of prophecy and latter-day revelation for guiding and inspiring them in coping with the problems of daily life.

Closely related to the problem of securing people's religious commitments, belief in prophecy and revelation are also highly important but arguably understudied topics in social science studies of religion. Thus, for example, religious scholar Rodney Stark emphasizes that while prophetic texts of the major monotheistic faith traditions (Judaism, Christianity, and Islam) are all believed by their adherents to be based on divine revelation, the question of how revelations actually occur has seldom been studied empirically: "To the extent that we cannot answer this question, we remain ignorant of the origins of our basic subject matter: religious culture."[20] In turn, transcendent claims of divine instruction and moral sanction channeled through purported revelations from God provide the strongest kind of justification for believers' compliance with religious requirements of sacrifice, renunciation of outsiders, and personal submission to group authority. We use the term *supernatural valence* to emphasize the ultimate value that Latter-day Saints attach to the authoritative claims and directives issued by their prophet-leaders, beginning with Joseph Smith. While not elevated to the stature of holy writ that guides the entire religious community, patriarchal blessings are charged with supernatural valence by individual Latter-day Saints through application of the blessings' content to their personal lives in ways that are consistent with and strongly reinforce LDS theological teachings. This conclusion is illustrated at length in chapters 5 and 6 by our statistical analysis of major doctrinal themes included in early patriarchal blessings.

Joseph Smith has been the subject of numerous biographies that have been either debunking or hagiographic in their analyses and conclusions.[21] The ultimate question—whether Smith was an authentic prophet of God or a religious fraud—appears irresistible to most students of Mormonism. The issue of prophetic authenticity cannot, of course, be separated from peoples' underlying religious orientations and belief in a transcendent deity. For religious believers in the monotheistic traditions of Judaism, Christianity, and Islam, the distinction between true prophets empowered by God and false prophets who have no such commission, but are considered deluded or seek to deceive for personal gain, is of crucial importance. Nonbelievers or detached scholars of these same traditions tend to dismiss or bracket the question of divine empowerment, but they consider seriously a designated prophet's sincerity, intentions, and positive or negative social legacy. As Reid Neilson and Terryl Givens remark in their introduction to *Joseph Smith, Jr.: Reappraisals After Two Centuries*, "a variety of interpretive strategies can bypass this question [authentic prophet or fraud] in order to explore Smith's influence, historical impacts, parallels with literary figures, and situatedness in new religious contexts."[22]

Furthermore, while scholarly focus on the peculiar charismatic qualities of religious founders hailed as prophets by their disciples is perfectly understandable, less attention has been paid to the *social process* in which prophetic religious movements emerge and develop. Recent studies, however, including some concerning the doctrinal development of early Mormonism, have begun to shift attention to the proclamation and promulgation of divine revelation as a consequence of social interaction between multiple religious actors in particular historical and cultural contexts.[23] This, we think, represents a more realistic and comprehensive approach to understanding the role of prophecy and revelation in the emergence and subsequent development of new religious movements. By focusing attention on the blessings issued by early LDS church patriarchs, we not only want to highlight the commitment function these blessings served (and continue to serve in the contemporary LDS Church) but also spotlight their contribution to the prophetic development of early Mormonism as an American frontier religion.

If and when new religions claiming a divine mandate conveyed through prophetic oracles become institutionally stable, organizational controls predictably emerge over time that impose constraints on new doctrinal revelations or prophetic edicts. Inherently unstable in its pure form, the strong charisma of oracular prophecy typically is modified and contained within institutional structures over time, allowing the more predictable forms of traditional and legal authority to take root and develop.[24] Ironically, the organizational containment or even suppression of charismatic impulses in religious traditions as they age may have the unintended consequence of alienating subsequent generations of adherents who perceive institutionalized religious forms to be calcified, impersonal, uninspiring, or even corrupted by a largely self-interested professional clergy.[25] Consequently, some people raised within prophetic religious traditions may conclude that the formalized expressions of faith in their societies no longer adequately address their spiritual or existential concerns. These people constitute a potential market of religious seekers for whom spiritual reformation and a renewal of charisma, including direct revelatory guidance (rather than the strictures imposed by a professional clergy), may have strong appeal. Such a market for revealed religion was already in place when the religiously untutored Joseph Smith Jr. astonished his upstate New York neighbors and contemporaries with claims of having obtained a new scripture that heralded, in ultra-supernatural language, a religious restoration and the imminent second coming of Jesus Christ.

RESTORATIONISM AND THE CHARISMATIC
APPEAL OF EARLY MORMONISM

Mormonism emerged in antebellum America along with other restorationist groups, such as the Disciples of Christ, Church (or Churches) of Christ, and, later, Seventh-day Adventists and Jehovah's Witnesses. Antedating the restorationist movement were Christian "primitivists," such as the Anabaptists and Quakers, who held a common goal of reestablishing Christianity in its original, primitive form. Thus the religious restoration proclaimed in early Mormonism was a singular manifestation of a larger Christian restoration movement in both England and the United States.[26] Various eighteenth- and nineteenth-century restorationist groups rejected the doctrinal and ecclesiastical formalism of creedal Christianity. Many restorationists emphasized New Testament lay community and spiritual gifts that ostensibly enhanced ordinary believers' personal access to supernatural aid and divine guidance in their daily lives. Early Mormon converts in particular—women as well as men—were Christian "primitivists" who longed for a restoration of the primitive apostolic church and its charismatic claim to spiritual gifts, especially the gift of prophecy and contemporary revelation.[27] Visionary, spirit-centered religion also appealed to Methodists of that era (including Brigham Young and his brothers) who were exponents of a frontier faith that specialized in organizing mass revival meetings that attracted tens of thousands of religious seekers and remorseful sinners.[28] In his influential analysis of the organizational development of early Mormonism, Michael Quinn argues that many early converts were attracted to the Mormon restoration precisely because of its initial nonhierarchical emphasis on the lay "priesthood of all believers."[29]

What was distinctive about the Latter-day Saint restoration was the charismatic appeal of Joseph Smith's claims to have been empowered by God and the intervention of angels to translate an ancient scriptural record—published in 1830 as the Book of Mormon. It was their yearning for God's direct, personal guidance in their lives and the messianic fulfillment of biblical prophecies concerning the last days of human history that made Mormon converts receptive to the Book of Mormon.[30] Upon publication, the Book of Mormon became an objective religious artifact, consisting of 531 pages of biblical language that sustained a complex prophetic narrative of ancient American civilizations and their relationship to the resurrected Christ. In typical oracular fashion, the Book of Mormon compelled readers to either accept or reject its authority as God's word to authentic seekers of religious truth. It was, of course, the Book of Mormon that immediately generated the widespread appellation by which the Latter-day Saints became widely, and often derisively, known.

Even more compelling to early Mormons than the Book of Mormon was Joseph Smith himself, who not only claimed God's gift as a seer and translator of ancient scriptural records but charismatically enacted the role of a living prophet as well. His religiously provocative claims were, of course, also highly controversial and immediately constituted the primary grounds of energetic opposition to the new religion. Restorationists who were drawn to Smith's professions of supernatural empowerment and divine favor were in need of both organizational and doctrinal direction. These soon were provided through a stream of oracular revelations attributed to God, as channeled through the youthful Joseph Smith, and first published in 1833 as the Book of Commandments.[31] Unlike the Book of Mormon, which was proclaimed by Smith to be a divinely aided translation of ancient records that had been miraculously conveyed to him, Smith's contemporary revelations were claimed to be direct messages from God in response to his prayerful queries on a variety of current, pressing issues. These direct revelations were supplemented with additional visionary writings that elaborated significantly on biblical passages (i.e., the Book of Moses, the Book of Abraham, and the Vision of Enoch), introducing a number of theological innovations.[32]

As Jan Shipps and other scholars of early Mormon history make clear, in contrast to its more conventional restoration themes concerning the primitive gospel and organization of the apostolic church, the later and more radical aspects of LDS salvation theology were implicitly embedded in some of Joseph Smith's earliest pronouncements, both prior to and after publication of the Book of Mormon.[33] The gradual exposition of the most radical doctrines of the Mormon restoration became progressively divisive, causing rifts not only between Mormons and their neighbors but also within the Mormon community. The rapid formation of Mormon organizational authority and escalating doctrinal innovation were stumbling blocks for some of Smith's earliest followers, generating dissension and defections, but these institutional developments also provided Mormonism with essential intellectual and organizational coherence as a new religious movement under constant attack by both religious and secular detractors. Smith's organizational revelations produced what converts welcomed as the restored Church of Jesus Christ. His increasingly radical doctrinal revelations constituted what his most loyal followers embraced as the "fullness" of the restored gospel. Concomitantly, Smith's rapidly expanding cadre of lay disciples conceded him the status of God's latter-day prophet, seer, and revelator.[34] The Mormon restoration thus had its prophet, and the foundation of his appeal to many nineteenth-century religious seekers in both America and Europe was the promise of direct contact with and guidance from the living God through modern revelation.

While Joseph Smith dominated the organizational and doctrinal development of the restored church of Jesus Christ and was its star attraction, it would be a great oversimplification to conclude that his prophetic voice alone set the course for a new religion on the American frontier. Successful new religions always depend on the convergence of like-minded individuals who willingly combine their material and intellectual resources in the process of mutually constructing a distinctive moral community and the necessary institutions for sustaining it.[35] A prophetic figure who is also the founder of what proves to be an enduring religious tradition needs capable lieutenants who have learned to speak the same religious language and have leadership potential. Early Mormon converts already believed in supernatural manifestations of power, spiritual gifts, and the need for contemporary prophetic guidance. The language of Christian primitivism and restorationism was widespread on the American frontier at the time of Smith's publication of the Book of Mormon—a language that early Mormon converts and subsequent leaders such as Oliver Cowdery, the Whitmer brothers, Joseph Knight and his sons, Parley P. Pratt, Edward Partridge, Newell K. Whitney, Orson Hyde, Thomas Marsh, William W. Phelps, Frederick G. Williams, and especially Sidney Rigdon already shared.[36] Many of these men were already religiously opinionated and, in comparison to Joseph Smith's rudimentary secular and religious education, were relatively well versed in the religious controversies of their day. These and many other early converts had varying degrees of influence on the religious imagination of the relatively untutored Joseph Smith (who nonetheless absorbed and synthesized novel ideas very quickly), and they helped contribute to forming the fledgling church and the innovation of its emerging doctrines.[37] All were united by their belief in biblical restorationism and the gift of prophecy—not only as authoritatively exercised by their fledgling prophet, but also as a gift universally available to members of the restored church.

In Mormonism's early years, both male and female converts exercised what they believed were spiritual gifts, including speaking in tongues, interpreting tongues, healing the sick, casting out devils, and prophesying in the name of the Lord.[38] Through democratic lay participation in offering public prayers, preaching sermons (male prerogatives in the nineteenth century), pronouncing various blessings upon their families and fellow Latter-day Saints, and proclaiming the restored gospel to their neighbors, early Mormon converts shared, cultivated, and contributed to a common religious vocabulary for expressing the emerging principles and doctrines of a new religious faith. Smith regularly sought advice and support from counselors. He collaborated doctrinally with—and was significantly influenced by—close lieutenants in an increasingly complex ecclesiastical hierarchy of lay priesthood offices that required participatory leadership in every organizational unit of the church. Upon ordination to various priesthood offices, male converts immediately became part of a rapidly expanding leadership cadre who believed themselves, like their prophet, empowered to act and speak in the name of God. While subject to the superior authority of periodic church conferences, newly formed councils, and ultimately to Joseph Smith's oracular revelations as First Elder and President of the High Priesthood, ordinary church members expected to receive personal revelations and be inspired through the ministrations of God's Spirit in the performance of their lay church duties and assignments.

Among those whose influence was particularly significant in the unfolding of Joseph's Smith's prophetic career were his mother, father, and brothers—especially (before an untimely death) his oldest brother, Alvin, and subsequently his next-oldest brother, Hyrum.[39] Quite obviously, familial ties were of great importance to the young prophet, who initially received crucial support from parents and siblings and subsequently endowed his brothers with various priesthood positions in the emerging ecclesiastical councils of the church.[40] Hyrum was ordained a high priest in 1831 and was subsequently elevated to the positions of counselor to the president in 1837 and assistant president of the church in 1841. Joseph's younger brothers Samuel, William, and Don Carlos were all ordained elders and advanced to the office of high priest soon after the Church of Christ was organized in 1830. Samuel subsequently was called to serve on the Kirtland High Council in 1834, William was ordained as an apostle in 1835, and Don Carlos was appointed as president of the Kirtland high priests' quorum in 1836. And, in 1833, Joseph Jr. bestowed upon his father, Joseph Sr., the office of church patriarch.[41]

The primary duty of the church patriarch was to bless the people by laying his hands upon their heads and issuing them individual, personal blessings in the name of Jesus Christ. Invoking prophetic revelation, the patriarch typically (1) offered summary assessments of blessing recipients' religious motives and moral character; (2) foretold their elect participation in the culminating events of the last days preparatory to Christ's eagerly anticipated, apocalyptic second coming; (3) admonished them to remain steadfast in their commitment to the restored church; and (4) pronounced a variety of both material and spiritual blessings in their lives as compensation for the sacrifices required of them in furthering the work of the latter-day restoration. Significantly, as an essential part of the "restoration of all things," the patriarch also (5) prophetically discerned recipients' lineage as descendants of the Twelve Tribes of Israel, making Mormon converts covenantal heirs of Zion and partakers of God's promises to his chosen people.[42] Finally, and most significantly, faithful church members (6) were promised salvation and eternal life in the celestial Kingdom of God, reassuring them of the supreme fulfillment and reward for their sacrificial dedication.

In the next chapter we offer a brief synopsis of early LDS history, emphasizing both the religious excitement and the opposition stimulated by Joseph Smith's prophetic claims. Subsequently, in chapter 3 we further describe and discuss the commitment function of early patriarchal blessings, especially the way in which the office of the patriarch operated in conjunction with Mormonism's restorationist belief in contemporary prophecy and revelation.

UNITY AND CONFLICT IN EARLY MORMON HISTORY

The rise of nineteenth-century Mormonism illustrates the important convergence of heretical religious innovation, primary group social reinforcement, and auspicious historical circumstances involving a receptive religious market in the context of a supportive cultural environment. All of these elements, in potent combination, are conducive to the successful emergence of new religious traditions.[1] In the case of the Mormons, the heretical innovator was Joseph Smith Jr. The initial social reinforcement came through Smith's attentive, if not doting, parents and siblings and a spreading network of credulous neighbors and employers. Historical circumstances included American political separation of church and state and frontier settings in a new nation ripe with uncharted democratic possibilities for innovation, expansion, and change. The supportive cultural environment included both the regional folk magic traditions of New England and upstate New York, as well as the camp meeting revivals of the second Great Awakening that emphasized ultra-supernatural religion and ecstatic conversion.[2]

At the same time, we should not forget that the emergence of new religions typically generates discord and divisions as well as spiritual fulfillment for believers. Detractors typically characterize adherents of new religions as deluded—and their leaders as unscrupulous villains. Prophetic new religions predictably struggle, too, with internal doubts and dissent. In the context of mass Mormon migrations from western New York to the American Midwest and ultimately to Utah's Rocky Mountain Great Basin, we highlight here those aspects of early Mormon history that demonstrate the polarizing effects of new religious movements founded in the strong charisma of oracular prophecy.

NEW YORK

Joseph Smith Jr. was born in Sharon, Vermont, but at the age of eleven, he moved with his family to Palmyra, New York, in the winter of 1816–17. Palmyra was one of a string of towns and villages in upstate New York that blossomed along the length of the Erie Canal between Albany and Buffalo during the first quarter of the nineteenth century. Propertyless after experiencing a series of financial reversals in New England, Joseph Smith Sr. hoped to begin anew in the expanding frontier economy of western New York.[3] Both Smith parents were deeply religious, Bible-reading literalists, but they were divided by an important difference: Joseph's mother, Lucy, was "churched" (uniting with the Presbyterians, circa 1824), but his father, Joseph Sr., was not affiliated and, in fact, was antagonistic toward organized religion. At the same time, Joseph Sr. professed vision-like dreams whose meanings eluded and troubled him, and he allowed the pious Lucy to have primary control over their children's religious upbringing. Joseph Smith Sr. was reasonably well educated for his time and place and, prior to moving to New York, had tried his hand at teaching school as well as farming and tending a store. In New York he cleared land and again attempted farming; Lucy sold assorted homemade items and refreshments, which she and the children peddled from a cart, for extra income. Along with other men in the Palmyra area, Joseph Sr. also believed in occult powers and joined with some of his neighbors in deploying magical artifices in the search for buried treasure, an occupation in which Joseph Jr. also engaged as a young man.

Of Joseph Jr., only a smattering of detail is known of his childhood and early adolescence (most of which comes from his mother's memoir, written in old age after Joseph's death).[4] Joseph suffered a serious infection in his leg as a child, was partially lame for a period of time following a horrific operation, and consequently appears to have been the object of his mother's particular attention and affection. Other than a slight limp, Joseph outgrew his childhood handicap and, like his father and five brothers, developed a strong, broad-shouldered physique and a mature height in excess of six feet.[5] We can infer from various contemporary sources that as a young man he was bright, literate (though the recipient of only a very sporadic grammar-school education), sociable, imaginative, and, apparently like his father, an able storyteller with a narrative talent. That as a man he would be capable of entertaining radical theological ideas, authoring and/or "translating" foundational religious texts—and grow to be the charismatic leader of an enduring religious movement—would have been (and was) unfathomable to his rural Palmyra contemporaries.

According to his own history, in response to the competitive spirit of revivalism in the Palmyra area, young Joseph developed serious religious concerns at about the age of fourteen, which led to his first supernatural religious experience. In later life, Joseph described this as a literal encounter with God the Father and Jesus Christ, who directly spoke to him and resolved his religious anxieties.[6] In both his and his mother's later accounts of these experiences, he was immediately supported by his family rather than ridiculed for claiming to have been favored by celestial visions. However, Joseph also reported that he was deeply disappointed when his relation of the incident was summarily dismissed by a respected revivalist preacher in whom he confided his story. Other religious seekers in the same cultural environs prayed for and claimed visions of God and Jesus Christ; why not Joseph? Several years passed with no apparent validation of his first vision until, at the age of eighteen, young Joseph reported receiving another celestial visitation. This time, he said, an angel appeared to him, informing him of the existence of ancient records inscribed on gold plates, long hidden in a nearby hill; it would be his privilege to unearth and translate them.

In Joseph's account, though, the angel forbade him to remove the plates from their location until four years had passed. Ostensibly this probationary period would allow Joseph to achieve a more mature understanding of his prophetic calling and corresponding religious responsibilities. Following his elopement with Emma Hale in 1827, Joseph announced that he finally had been given God's permission to retrieve the ancient records and begin his supernaturally aided translation. In the meantime, rumors had been rife in the area about Joseph's possession of the gold plates, and men who previously had employed or worked with the Smiths in treasure-digging ventures felt entitled to their share of the gold. Pursued and threatened by these men, Joseph found it necessary to flee Palmyra and take up residence with Emma's skeptical parents in Harmony, Pennsylvania, just over the New York–Pennsylvania state line.

As with his previous visionary announcement, Joseph's own parents and siblings (especially his two older brothers, Alvin and Hyrum) expressed not the slightest doubt or criticism concerning his divinely appointed possession of the golden records and were completely support-ive of his emerging prophetic identity. They quickly had come to accept Joseph as God's supernaturally anointed agent for bringing about a great and marvelous work, one whose ultimate purpose was yet to be revealed. For eighteen months, Joseph struggled with the translation of what was to become the Book of Mormon. Emma sometimes served as a scribe for Joseph's translation (or transcription) of the plates through his personal "seer stone" and the "Urim and Thummim," ancient Hebrew prophetic devices that, according to Joseph, were hidden along with the gold plates.[7] But Joseph's principal scribe during this time—and the financier for the translation project—was a prosperous Palmyra farmer, Martin Harris, who combined Yankee business practicality with religious credulity and an eccentric personality. The work of transcription was going slowly, and then Harris proceeded to lose 116 manuscript pages of painstaking dictation. At an agonizing standstill for six months, the work was suddenly rejuvenated and completed with amazing speed upon the appearance of Oliver Cow-dery, who had boarded with the Smiths in Palmyra and heard of Joseph's heavenly visitations and the gold plates. At the time of his conversion and subsequent secretarial labor as scribe for Joseph's renewed dictation of the Book of Mormon, Cowdery was a twenty-two-year-old schoolteacher who shared the Smith family's ultra-supernatural worldview and possessed good writing and language skills.[8]

The Book of Mormon, named after an alleged ancient American prophet (identified in the Book of Mormon itself as the person responsible for preserving the records of his people), was published in March 1830. A scant month later, in April, Joseph Smith organized what was initially called the Church of Christ. Conversion to the new church spread through family networks. In addition to Oliver Cowdery, Martin Harris, and Joseph Smith's own family, the first members included other sympathetic fami-lies who had supported Joseph during his "transcription" of the plates. Particularly supportive in this regard were the Knight family (by whom Joseph previously had been employed) and the Whitmers (introduced to Joseph by Oliver Cowdery). Among the witnesses who attested to the supernatural provenance of the Book of Mormon upon its publication were Cowdery, Harris, three Smiths, and five Whitmers, plus a Whitmer son-in-law.

Other neighbors in the area, however, became increasingly hostile to the fledgling religion. Opposition came from men still angry about their perceived lost investments of time and money in fruitless treasure-seeking ventures, local clergymen and their religiously adamant flocks, and Emma's irate father—all of whom considered Joseph to be a shiftless charlatan and his followers to be ignorant dupes. The new church began to suffer hectoring and threatening disruptions of its religious services, and Joseph was served with harrying lawsuits on charges of being an imposter and a disorderly person. Though vexatious at the time, these initial oppositional efforts to discredit and thwart the new faith in New York were relatively mild obstacles compared to the violence that lay in store for later believers in Ohio and the frontier communities of Missouri and Illinois.

OHIO

Constantly reinforced in his prophetic role by persistent queries from his followers concerning God's designs for them, Joseph responded with oracular instructions to proselytize for the new faith, sending them out in pairs to disseminate the Book of Mormon, proclaim the restoration of the Church of Jesus Christ in the world's last days through the authority of divine revelation, and baptize all who would listen to and accept their message. From the outset of its history as a new religion, Mormonism was continually bolstered by its members' commitment to aggressive, often highly sacrificial yet ultimately productive recruitment efforts. Among those who came into early contact with the Mormon restoration movement through the widespread missionary distribution of the Book of Mormon were Brigham Young (who read a copy shortly after its publication in 1830 but waited to join the new church until 1832) and Sidney Rigdon, who was a mature, well-regarded "Reformed Baptist" (Disciples of Christ) minister in Mentor, Ohio.[9] Rigdon received his copy of the Book of Mormon from Oliver Cowdery and Parley P. Pratt (an erstwhile Rigdon acolyte), who had been sent from New York by young Joseph Smith (then twenty-four years of age) on a "Lamanite" (Indian) mission to Missouri. At first skeptical, Rigdon converted in little more than a week, abjectly renounced his pulpit, and hastened to New York to see for himself the youthful latter-day prophet and to discern the portents of his own religious future.

We can only imagine Joseph Smith's reaction to the news of Rigdon's conversion and expedition to see him in rural New York. Rigdon was twelve years Joseph's senior, a serious Bible student, and a famous preacher in the Ohio Western Reserve. It is not apparent, however, that the young prophet ever felt intimidated by the older, more experienced man. Alternatively, we can surmise that the formally untutored Smith made a strong impression on Rigdon, and that Smith reciprocally recognized that Rigdon's religious stature was a tremendous resource to the as-yet-underdeveloped religious enterprise set in motion by the publication of the Book of Mormon. Here was a golden opportunity for Joseph to radically expand his prophetic vision, and he seized it. Within weeks of Rigdon's arrival, Joseph promulgated revelations worded in the voice of God, instructing the beleaguered band of New York disciples to uproot themselves with all their worldly possessions and "assemble together at the Ohio" to receive "my law" and be "endowed with power from on high."[10] The first Mormon migration in search of a hallowed place, in which the Latter-day Saints could prosper and perfect their religion, was under way.

In and around Kirtland, Ohio, not far from the shores of Lake Erie and the present-day suburbs of Cleveland, Joseph Smith and his New York followers found several hundred religious seekers, including newly baptized Latter-day Saints, waiting in eager anticipation to see the prophet. They were New Testament Christian "primitivists"—former followers of Sidney Rigdon and/or adherents of local Disciples of Christ congregations. Many of them, like Rigdon, had been converted through the earlier proselytizing mission of Cowdery and Pratt. Within less than a year, Mormon missionary work was flourishing in the Ohio Western Reserve. At a special conference of elders gathered to approve publication of Joseph's revelations, God's words to Mormon converts, as channeled through the prophet, were: "Hearken, O Ye people of my church. . . . They who go forth . . . to them is power given to seal both on earth and in heaven."[11]

With continued proselytizing in the region, Kirtland quickly became a Mormon stronghold. It was in Kirtland where, as Lavina Fielding Anderson puts it, "answers emerged to two critical questions: How does the church work? and What does it mean to be a Mormon?"[12] Joseph's first tasks were to assert his restraining control over the doctrinal beliefs and "enthusiastic" religious modes of expression that had flourished in Kirtland prior to his arrival, and to develop an organizational structure for the orderly regulation of church affairs. This was accomplished through scheduled conferences, the formation of councils and committees, and the reassuring directive guidance of a steady stream of oracular revelations. While the young prophet acted as a channel for the voice of God in response to the questions and concerns of the growing community of

Latter-day Saint converts in Ohio, various theological and authority issues were shaped through the mundane human work of discussion, debate, and approval by conference voting. Early Mormonism in Kirtland was both prophet-centered and congregational in its administrative mode of functioning.

Additionally, it was in Kirtland where Joseph announced the restoration of the "patriarchal priesthood" and the office of the patriarch, to which he ordained his father Joseph Sr. (of whom more will be said in chapter 3). Consequently, it was in Kirtland where Joseph Sr. experienced a dramatic reversal in his heretofore disappointing material fortunes and lowly social standing. Now surrounded by his five strapping sons, and bolstered by the respectful acknowledgment of the rapidly growing Latter-day Saint community, the elder Smith arguably savored the most satisfying moments of his adult life.

During the early days of the gathering to Kirtland, Joseph Smith Jr. and Sidney Rigdon also were preoccupied with producing an "inspired translation" of the Bible in which they presumed, through prayer and divine revelation, to clarify and correct ambiguous Bible passages and, if necessary, to enlarge the text with additional prophetic material. These shared meditations with Rigdon (who supplanted Cowdery as the prophet's scribe) played an important role in the more sophisticated development of Joseph's doctrinal understanding and religious imagination. Collaboration with Rigdon in scriptural exegesis served as a foundation for Smith's more radical theological innovations—especially those that came a decade later in Nauvoo, Illinois.

Along with questions about proper forms of religious worship, church governance, and doctrinal concerns, economic issues assumed immediate importance. In the spirit of primitive Christian equality and selfless brotherhood, a number of Kirtland converts had been drawn to communal sharing experiments prior to the arrival of Joseph's New York flock. Furthermore, Sidney Rigdon had preached in support of Christian communalism prior to becoming a Mormon and spokesman for the prophet. Many of the uprooted and now unemployed and landless New York disciples were on the verge of destitution for the sake of their new faith, and they needed material assistance. Adding to their poverty was the fact that many men among them were called to serve proselytizing missions, leaving their wives and families to depend on the kindness of others while they preached of the restored gospel. All of these factors played a role in the formulation of Joseph Smith's revelation concerning the "law of consecration," which stipulated economic cooperation rather than competitive striving as the foundation of Mormon efforts to build what they believed was foreordained to become the Kingdom of God on earth.

The law of consecration was particularly expected to be applied in the "land of Zion," which Joseph had identified, through oracular prophecy, as Jackson County, Missouri—a distance of eight hundred miles from Kirtland, on the eastern border of Indian Territory. According to revelation, in Zion, the Latter-day Saints would receive "an inheritance," which was understood to mean property and land for impoverished but faithful converts. Once gathered to Zion, they would build the New Jerusalem of the Kingdom of God on earth, practice the law of consecration, and live together in prosperous harmony, without rich or poor, while preparing to receive the second coming of the Messiah. In the end, these utopian aspirations and prophetically mandated plans for Joseph's devoted followers were never realized. Internal divisions and violence soon surfaced in Kirtland, and the Latter-day Saints who had been gathering to Missouri's Zion were about to experience a taste of frontier mobocracy.

In Mark Staker's words, "Violence and confrontation flared in Hiram at precisely the moment Joseph received some of his most significant revelations and made preparations to publish them."[13] Hiram, a village south of Kirtland, was home to a sizeable number of new Latter-day Saint converts, most of whom had been Methodists, Baptists, or affiliated with the Disciples of Christ and were well acquainted with Sidney Rigdon's earlier doctrinal preaching in the area. Many of these converts were eager to abide in their new faith and follow their prophet's counsel in all things—but not all. Some had quickly become disillusioned for an assortment of reasons. Among other things, Joseph's and Rigdon's efforts to "translate" the Bible deeply offended some. Contending Disciple preachers denounced the Smith-Rigdon visionary revelation concerning the destination of human souls to one of three "kingdoms," or degrees of glory in the afterlife, as a gross heresy; it radically departed from evangelical Christianity's bifurcation of heaven or hell as humanity's ultimate fate.[14] Adding strongly to the discord, relatives and neighbors of the many Mormons who were leaving or preparing to leave Ohio to gather with their follow Latter-day Saints in Jackson County, Missouri, felt alarm at the prospective human and material diminishment of their families and community.

In the early spring of 1832, a coordinated attack in the dark of night was made by twenty to thirty men on the residences of both Smith and Rigdon, who were living with their respective wives and children in Hiram while still engaged in their Bible translation work. The assailants were all former Mormons or had relatives who were. With murder in their hearts, they dragged the prophet and his scribe from their beds, but in the ensuing struggle and confusion they only succeeded in applying a hot coat of tar and feathers to their victims. Smith survived the attack with cracked ribs and a missing tooth; Rigdon suffered a brain concussion that left him delirious for several days. No one was ever charged or arrested for the assaults. Undeterred, and supported by faithful Latter-day Saints in both Ohio and Missouri, Joseph continued with his plans to publish the new revelations he had been receiving. The church's new press had been purchased and installed to operate in Independence, Missouri, in Jackson County.

Even though Kirtland was still in its infancy as the de facto Mormon headquarters, Independence had been identified through revelation as the gathering place for Zion. A temple site had been designated there (within a few blocks of Harry S. Truman's later home in Independence) to receive the Lord's second coming. Mormon population in the county was steadily increasing from an infusion of New York and Ohio members answering the call to gather in Zion. Nonmembers in the area—"Gentiles," to the increasingly embattled Latter-day Saints—became alarmed by the growing strength of the new settlers, many of whose New England origins and heretical religion clashed with the Southern mores of most Missourians. Slavery was a contentious issue, and Missouri slave owners quickly cast the Mormons as abolitionists.

In July 1833, violence erupted in Independence. The Mormons' print shop was attacked and ransacked by a mob; the press was destroyed; and the Mormon bishop in Zion, Edward Partridge, was tarred and feathered. The galleys of Joseph's Book of Commandments were strewn in the street. Implacable feelings rapidly escalated. In November, mob threats and further attacks forced Zion's Latter-day Saints to abandon their homes and the temple lot in Jackson County. Close to a thousand Mormon refugees spent the winter of 1833–34 shivering in makeshift shelters on the Missouri prairie.

After first advising legal means of addressing the Missouri crisis, the prophet's ultimate response was to raise a volunteer army of several hundred men in Kirtland and march a thousand miles through Indiana, Illinois, and Missouri to "redeem Zion" from her enemies. Plagued by poor planning, bickering, and mounting dissension along the way, "Zion's

Camp" was a tactical failure. A cholera outbreak decimated the Mormon "army," and, when confronted by a much larger Missouri militia mobilized to thwart the Mormon military threat, Joseph Smith prudently ordered the dissolution of Zion's Camp. Its volunteers straggled ingloriously back to Kirtland. Zion was not redeemed, and the Mormons' lost properties were never returned.

In Kirtland, Joseph was now forced to face charges by defecting members that he was a fallen prophet. In this perilous moment of his implausible prophetic career, we clearly see—and not for the first or last time —Smith's capacity for weathering a crisis of faith and even rebounding and fortifying his authority among his followers who had cause to repudiate him.[15] Often impetuous and headstrong in defending his personal honor, Joseph Smith also had a magnanimous character and knew how to inspire loyalty in times of risk and danger. Thus, following the debacle in Missouri, Smith's most ardent lieutenants (including Brigham Young) eventually emerged from among the ranks of Zion's Camp. Seven months after the failed Missouri expedition, conferences were convened in Kirtland whose business was to organize and designate members of two new priesthood leadership organizations: the Quorum of the Twelve Apostles and the First Quorum of the Seventy, with its seven presidents. Both groups were specifically charged with missionary responsibilities, and the membership of both groups consisted primarily of loyal veterans of Zion's Camp. Within another decade, the Twelve Apostles would assume leadership of the LDS Church, with Brigham Young at their head.

The spiritual apex of Kirtland's Mormon history came in March 1836, with the dedication of the Kirtland Temple. At great sacrifice of time, labor, and the Latter-day Saints' meager financial resources, the Kirtland Temple had been under construction for three years. Built on a hill west of the Chagrin River, the imposing temple was a 15,000-square-foot edifice of sandstone and brick covered with stuccoed plaster. Its walls stood 50 feet high, and its tower soared 110 feet above the ground. Considering the extent of Mormon poverty and lack of prior architectural knowledge, the finished temple was a remarkable achievement. Within its walls would assemble the various quorums of the priesthood, the School of the Prophets (for language and theological study), and the Kirtland High Council, as well as parents and their children for Sabbath services, patriarchal blessing meetings conducted by Father Smith, and various church conferences.

The weeks of ritual preparation leading up to the dedication of the temple and the dedication itself proved to be a massive exercise in Pentecostal catharsis. Tears of joy coursed freely, congregants claimed celestial visions, ministering angels were beheld, God was praised in unknown tongues, and the assembled quorums of the priesthood all voted by rising to their feet to sustain Brother Joseph as God's latter-day prophet. All told, hundreds, if not thousands, of people observed or participated in these events. As Richard Bushman notes, "These exhausting and exhilarating three months, the zenith of the Saints' ecstatic experience, came in the 1830s, at a high point of visionary religion in American history."[16] Thereafter, ecstatic forms of religious expression began to decline as a part of LDS worship, but faith in the ultra-supernatural foundations of the Mormon restoration did not. While praying in the temple a week after its dedication, Joseph Smith and Oliver Cowdery reported a vision of the Lord Jesus Christ's personal acceptance of "His House," followed, they claimed, by the appearance of Moses, Elias, and Elijah as celestialized beings—who bestowed upon Smith and Cowdery the "keys" of the respective priesthood dispensations these ancient prophets presumably represented.

It did not take long for the climate of spiritual endowment in Kirtland to dissipate, however. With economic storm clouds looming, Mormon leaders perceived the need to establish their own banking institution as a mechanism for paying mounting debt while continuing to fund ambitious land purchases, construction projects, church publication costs, and other cooperative enterprises of the restoration. The Kirtland Safety Society was established, and it began soliciting stockholders for investment funds to capitalize a banking establishment for the Mormon community. Sidney Rigdon and Joseph Smith were elected to serve as bank president and cashier, respectively.

Unfortunately, the formation of the Kirtland Safety Society coincided with a period of wild land speculation throughout the country, especially in the Ohio Western Reserve, that grossly inflated land values in the region. The national land bubble eventually burst and produced the economic panic of 1837, in which sound credit virtually evaporated, followed by a five-year depression that saw the failure of many banks and record-high unemployment levels.[17] Unchartered by the Ohio Legislature and underfunded to begin with, the Kirtland Safety Society collapsed, leaving its mostly Mormon investors with worthless paper notes for their hard specie deposits. The failure of the bank not only signaled financial ruin for the church but also generated a traumatic implosion of religious faith. Many followers now questioned the prophet's right to dictate in temporal as well as spiritual matters. After so many demands for personal sacrifice to sustain the Lord's work, how could a prophet of God have mismanaged their precious monetary resources so badly? The fury of disillusioned investors forced both Smith and Rigdon into hiding.

To illustrate the sharpness of division in the Kirtland Latter-day Saint community by September 1837, we quote Brigham Young's account of a meeting in the temple with leading church dissidents, as cited in Mark Staker's informative study of the Kirtland banking fiasco:

> The question before them was to ascertain how the Prophet Joseph could be deposed, and David Whitmer appointed President of the Church. . . . I rose up, and in a plain and forcible manner told them that Joseph was a Prophet . . . they could not destroy the appointment of the Prophet of God, they could only destroy their own authority . . . and sink themselves to hell. Many were highly enraged at my decided opposition to their measures, and Jacob Bump (an old pugilist) was so exasperated that he could not be still. . . . he writhed and twisted his arms and body saying, "How can I keep my hands off that man?" I told him if he thought it would give him any relief he might lay them on. This meeting was broken up without the apostates being able to unite on any decided measures of opposition. This was a crisis when earth and hell seemed [leagued] to overthrow the Prophet and Church of God. The knees of many of the strongest men in the Church faltered.[18]

Such angry scenes ensuing in the consecrated House of the Lord could scarcely have been imagined at the temple's joyful dedicatory services eighteen months earlier. A church conference voted to sustain the prophet and his counselors, but lawsuits multiplied, and more rebellious actions were being planned by the dissenters, who included Lyman Johnson and John Boynton—ordained apostles only two years before—along with Joseph Smith's Book of Mormon financier and early scribe, Martin Harris, and numerous other former stalwarts.

In desperate legal straits, and bolstered by several revelations from God, Smith and Rigdon slipped out of Kirtland at the outset of the New Year—January 1838—abandoning Kirtland and the temple to unite with Mormon colonists who had been flocking to Missouri since 1830–31. They were soon followed by their families and other devoted priesthood leaders, such as Brigham Young and a majority of the apostles. In July of that year, an organized company of more than eight hundred Latter-day Saints left

Kirtland for Missouri, and as Staker notes, the next six years saw continued emigration from Kirtland.[19] Its prophet gone, Kirtland quickly faded into small-town obscurity.

MISSOURI

Expelled by mobs from their homes in Jackson County in 1833, Missouri Mormons had regrouped and acquired land in Caldwell County, in the northwest region of the state, which had been set aside for them by the Missouri state legislature as a form of redress for their lost properties.[20] The Latter-day Saints' Missouri headquarters was relocated to a place they called Far West. In Far West, as in Independence and Kirtland, land was surveyed for a temple, and cornerstones were laid for a new House of the Lord. Designated as the seat of Caldwell County, Far West was now the center of Zion, and the prophet and his loyal Kirtland followers gathered here throughout the spring and summer of 1838. In escaping the divisions and financial woes of Kirtland, they arrived just in time to become extricated in a new hornet's nest, as intense hostility toward Mormons was again flaring up in Missouri. By 1838 Far West and environs had attracted approximately 5,000 Latter-day Saints, who began spilling over into the adjacent Carroll and Daviess Counties. Missourians in the area again became alarmed by the burgeoning Mormon presence, and old antipathies were rekindled. Conflict escalated with attacks on Mormon voters at election polls and raids on outlying Mormon farms. But this time, Mormons were prepared to retaliate: they met force with force, organizing their own militia units abetted by the Danites, a secret fraternal organization.

The Danites initially developed as a kind of vigilante group for stifling internal dissent. Their original policing mission appears to have been supported by both Rigdon and Smith, who had become highly sensitized to the personal dangers posed by disaffected members. In Far West, this group of alienated members included, jarringly, Oliver Cowdery and David and John Whitmer—three of Joseph Smith's earliest and most dedicated converts, all of whom had published their sworn testimonies regarding the authenticity of the Book of Mormon to commence the latter-day restoration movement. Cowdery (miffed, perhaps, at having been displaced by Rigdon as spokesman to the prophet) and the Whitmers objected to theocratic interference in their temporal affairs and political independence. They, along with other prominent Missouri church leaders William Phelps and Lyman Johnson, were targeted with threats from Danite zealots. The threats were given credence by Sidney Rigdon's June 1838 "Salt Sermon," in which he compared the dissenters to salt that had lost its savor and avowed that they would be "trodden under the foot of men."[21] These erstwhile church officials, now branded as traitors, fled the county and filed affidavits against their former brethren.

Rigdon's militant rhetoric fanned the flames of conflict with non-Mormons in the area as well. In another bellicose oration, this time on Independence Day, he exclaimed—to the cheers of a large crowd of Latter-day Saints in Far West—that if mobs again descended upon the Mormons, it would be "between us and them a war of extermination." Following depredations by Daviess County vigilantes against Mormon settlers soon after Rigdon's intemperate speech, Joseph Smith called for Mormon militia units to protect the Latter-day Saints throughout the region. Many prominent Danites and others went on the offensive, sacking and burning homes and stores in the county seat of Gallatin. Rumors were rampant that the Mormons were preparing to invade and destroy other "Gentile" towns in adjacent counties; reciprocally, the Mormons at Far West received exaggerated reports that a Missouri mob had captured and was preparing to execute several Latter-day Saint prisoners. An armed engagement ensued between Mormon military forces and a unit of the Missouri militia. Three Mormons and one Missouri militiaman were killed, and the Missourians were put to flight. Conflict between Mormons and the state of Missouri was spiraling out of control. Governor Lilburn Boggs issued an executive order that mimicked Rigdon's language of extermination, calling for militia troops to drive the Mormons from the state. Three days later, a 240-man militia unit attacked the Mormon settlement of Haun's Mill in eastern Caldwell County and massacred seventeen men and boys who had hurriedly congregated in the community blacksmith shop to defend themselves.

The Haun's Mill survivors, mostly women and children, fled to Far West for protection. Indeed, outlying Mormon settlements in the area were all abandoned, and their inhabitants poured into Far West to escape the wrath of their persecutors. On October 30, Latter-day Saints awoke to see an encamped army of 2,500 men on the outskirts of Far West. Armed with artillery and the governor's extermination order, commanding general Samuel Lucas (an old enemy, heavily involved in the first forced eviction of Mormons from Independence) demanded both the surrender of the city and designated Mormon leaders, most especially Joseph Smith and Sidney Rigdon. The following day the prophet capitulated; he was summarily sentenced, by a hastily organized court-martial, to be executed by firing squad on a charge of treason and an assortment of other alleged crimes. His life precariously in the balance, Smith was saved by militia general Alexander Doniphan, who refused to carry out the order of his superior officer, calling it "cold-blooded murder" and adding, "if you execute these men, I will hold you responsible before an earthly tribunal, so help me God."[22]

His immediate death averted, Smith, along with a handful of other Mormon leaders, was bound over to civil authorities in Richmond, Missouri, for arraignment. The prisoners were subsequently transported to Liberty Jail in nearby Clay County to await trial. In the meantime, the state's militia occupied Far West. The Latter-day Saints were again expelled from their homes and warned never to return. Confiscation of their properties was justified as reimbursement for the cost of mobilizing the militia to defend the rights of Missouri citizens.

At this point in their history, one might ask, What had the decade-long millenarian gathering to Zion accomplished for the Latter-day Saints? Disillusionment, death, and destitution were certainly among the most obvious outcomes. Many faltered and left the church. But, amazingly, large numbers remained steadfast in their commitment and faith in the latter-day restoration. Understanding this kind of religious devotion, in the face of remorseless opposition and defeat, requires an examination of the underlying ideational, organizational, and social commitments that characterize enduring new religions. For the Latter-day Saints, it was a time for new leaders to step forward and guide the bewildered faithful to a rejuvenated sense of purpose and their ultimate destiny. Having ascended to a senior position in the Quorum of the Twelve, Brigham Young demonstrated his own tenacity and practicality as he and other rising apostles, such as Heber C. Kimball and John Taylor, assumed responsibility for directing the outcasts' long retreat from the hostile Missouri frontier to refuge on the Illinois side of the Mississippi River.

ILLINOIS

Illinois towns along the banks of the Mississippi, including Quincy, the county seat of Adams County, sympathetically welcomed the exiled Mormons.[23] The prophet and others who faced charges with him were still languishing without bond or trial in jail in Liberty, Missouri, but Sidney Rigdon had been released on the grounds of ill health and joined other church members congregating in Quincy. In Joseph Smith's absence, the apostles and other church leaders were undecided on a course of action. But in late April 1839—suddenly, miraculously, joyously—Smith rode into Quincy. After six months in jail, Smith and the other Mormon prisoners had escaped in apparent collusion with some of their jailers, who had become increasingly embarrassed by the public outcry against Mormon persecution. The prophet swiftly reasserted his command of the church's emerging prospects in Illinois: "Two days after his arrival, a [church] council commissioned him to locate land on the west bank of the Mississippi and urged the Saints to move to the town of Commerce on the Illinois side. The Saints were to gather as before, with Commerce at the center."[24] Fifty-odd miles upriver from Quincy, Commerce was a sparsely inhabited spot on the map whose development had been severely hampered by its location in a swampy, malarial area that paralleled a horseshoe bend on the great river's eastern shoreline. Mormons immediately began to settle the unpromising river bottomlands and surrounding countryside as a gathering place to build anew the City of God. At first Smith himself described the site as a "wilderness." Later, in an optimistic flight of prophetic vision, he renamed the emerging city Nauvoo—a Hebrew word he had learned in Kirtland's School of the Prophets—meaning "beautiful location" and, he said, "carrying with it also the idea of rest."[25]

The rapid rise of Nauvoo on the banks of the Mississippi was a truly remarkable achievement for the impoverished Latter-day Saints, who had lost virtually everything they possessed in their flights from Kirtland and Far West. Within five years the expanding Mormon population in and around Nauvoo—12,000 to 15,000 people—equaled or exceeded that of the state capital in Springfield, where young Abraham Lincoln was beginning his career in Illinois law and state politics. Both brick and wood-frame homes had been erected, with outbuildings, gardens, orchards, and grazing areas geometrically laid out on a orderly grid conforming to Smith's "plat of Zion." A steamboat landing was in operation, and a hotel and other community buildings, including a Masonic lodge, had been built or were under construction. Numerous commercial and industrial enterprises had commenced doing business, and outlying farms were raising crops in the rich Illinois loam. The city supported two newspapers and had plans for a university. And on a commanding bluff overlooking the residential center of Nauvoo, construction was well under way on a new temple—much larger and more elaborate than Kirtland's—whose rising white-plastered limestone walls could be seen for miles, from the western Iowa shore and both north and south on the Mississippi River, as construction proceeded for four years.

Upon their arrival, though, the Nauvoo Saints first lived in tents, shanties, and log cabins. The settlers were smitten with cholera, malaria, and typhoid fever. A healthy community could only be sustained after the pestiferous swampland around Nauvoo was properly drained, at the cost of considerable time and cooperative effort. At the same time, many of the city's most able men—including the apostles Brigham Young, Wilford Woodruff, Heber C. Kimball, and Parley P. Pratt—were called away to serve proselytizing missions in the British Isles. While missed at home, their astonishingly successful missionary efforts among the British working class produced thousands of new converts, the majority of whom sailed to America to gather with and bolster their fellow Latter-day Saints in the city of Nauvoo. It was during Nauvoo's first difficult year of primitive living, construction, and expansion that Joseph Smith Sr. died, at age sixty-nine. Gathering his wife and children around him on his deathbed, he blessed them and ordained Hyrum, his oldest living son, as his successor to the office of church patriarch.[26] This gave Hyrum unprecedented standing as both patriarch and assistant president of the church, subordinate in authority only to the prophet, his younger brother.[27]

A year following Joseph Smith's escape from Missouri and return to the prophetic helm of Mormon leadership, John C. Bennett, quartermaster general of the Illinois state militia, professed conversion to the religion of the Latter-day Saints and ingratiated himself with Joseph Smith in Nauvoo.[28] Through Bennett's aid and political connections in the state, the Mormons were able to win approval of a city charter from the Illinois legislature, which granted Nauvoo, among other things, a municipal court and an independent militia unit, with arms and equipment supplied by the state. Consequently, Bennett was elected as Nauvoo's first mayor and installed as an assistant president in the First Presidency of the Church—a sudden appointment that conceivably troubled Sidney Rigdon and other Mormon veterans in the priesthood hierarchy. In the meantime, Joseph Smith Jr., prophet, seer, and revelator of the Church of Jesus Christ of Latter-day Saints, was commissioned by Governor Thomas Carlin as lieutenant general of the two- to three-thousand-man-strong Nauvoo Legion.[29] From facing the prospect of a firing squad and enduring on rations in a Missouri dungeon, Joseph had catapulted to generalship of the largest organized military force in Illinois—a presumably potent deterrent to future persecution. In the end, however, the Legion would not save him from being mobbed again in 1844.

As Nauvoo rapidly grew and prospered, portents of new trouble constantly surfaced. Missouri officials repeatedly attempted to extradite Smith to stand trial for charges pending against him in Missouri, but the Nauvoo municipal court would not bind the prophet over to arresting officers. In addition, Smith was accused of ordering an assassination attempt on Lilburn Boggs, who had issued the extermination order against the Mormons. The accusation further inflamed public opinion against Smith and the Nauvoo Saints. Both the Democratic and Republican parties of Illinois, moreover, felt frustrated by Smith's vacillating politics and consequently by their failures to secure the Mormon vote—which, since Mormons tended to follow their leaders' recommendations and vote as a bloc, was becoming a vexing political issue in the region.

The neighboring towns of Carthage and Warsaw were first suspicious and then baleful in their opposition to the theocratic advancement of Nauvoo under the prophecy-based authority of its leaders. With each new arrival of European converts swelling the boundaries of Nauvoo, the Mormons appeared well on their way to achieving economic and political control of the surrounding countryside. Outsiders nursed a number of complaints about their new Mormon neighbors: their religion was a fraudulent heresy; they professed democracy but practiced theocracy; their courts were biased against the interests of non-Mormons and subverted the independent authority of the judiciary; and they held in contempt the legal authority of non-Mormon officials. So alleged their enemies. The question, for many, was when and how the Mormons would be resisted or constrained. Increasingly hostile editorials in the *Warsaw Signal*, the nearest neighboring town newspaper, advocated mob violence. And, adding explosive tinder to growing fears and smoldering resentments, the doctrine and practice of plural marriage—formulated in Joseph Smith's private thinking as early as 1831—was becoming an open secret.

Feeling increasing pressure from Emma Smith's adamant refusal to countenance polygamy as either doctrine or practice, Joseph finally dictated a revelation in 1843 concerning "celestial marriages," which were validated both on earth and in heaven by the sealing authority of the restored priesthood. Most significantly, the prophet's revelation on celestial marriage included a man's religious duty, in a solemn covenant, to have marital relations with multiple wives.[30] In Nauvoo, the prophet not

only commenced teaching the doctrine of celestial marriage to an inner
circle of his most trusted supporters, but he also, in secret, began performing plural marriages for others while taking numerous additional wives
for himself.[31] Such a violation of conventional Christian teachings and
European-American marital mores in a tight-knit frontier community like
Nauvoo could hardly be concealed for long. When unofficially circulated,
news of the doctrine of plural marriage would scandalize and further out-
rage the Mormons' Gentile enemies and likewise drive a wedge through
the heart of the Latter-day Saint community.

Prior to his revelation on plural marriage, Joseph had pronounced other
prophetic doctrines in Nauvoo concerning temple sealing ordinances and
proxy baptisms on behalf of the dead, which were deemed radical heresies
by his critics but counted as crucial additions to the "restoration of all
things" by his most loyal followers. Then, in a publicly embarrassing (and
highly damaging) turn of events, the cynical and indiscreet John C. Bennett was excommunicated from the church by the Nauvoo High Council
in 1842 for multiple acts of adultery. Compelled to resign his posts as
mayor of Nauvoo (Joseph was elected in his stead) and general in the Nauvoo Legion, Bennett proceeded to become a bitter antagonist against the
Mormon community, and he did much to poison public opinion further
against the prophet and the Nauvoo Saints. His self-exculpatory characterization of covenantal celestial marriage as "spiritual wifery" and a form of
free love, sanctioned for both men and women by Joseph Smith, helped
indelibly link Mormon marriage doctrines with sexual promiscuity in the
popular imagination.

Even among the most faithful Latter-day Saints, the new doctrine of
plural marriage was difficult to receive and accept, though a large number
eventually did so. For others, however, including some of Nauvoo's most
prominent citizens, it was perceived as an abomination in the sight of God
and as stark evidence that Joseph Smith had become a fallen prophet.
Chief among the new dissenters were William Marks, president of the
Nauvoo Stake,[32] and William Law, a prosperous merchant who had ascended rapidly in the church hierarchy to become Joseph's second counselor in the First Presidency. Like the earlier dissenters in Kirtland, Marks
and Law were also opposed to theocratic intervention in business ventures.

While the dissent movement from within voiced open defiance of the
prophet's newest teachings and authority, the tone of anti-Mormon forces
in surrounding communities was becoming increasingly shrill and men-
acing. In April 1844, Smith took advantage of a general conference as a

means to unify the membership of the church behind him and his policies. Leading dissenters were deliberately excluded from participation at the conference, which minimized the possibility of an open and divisive debate. Preliminary speakers were called on to rebut criticism and accusations against the prophet and to defend his status as God's mouthpiece to the people. Smith himself then took the speaker's rostrum and delivered one of his last public discourses—ostensibly the funeral sermon for a certain King Follett, who had recently been killed in a construction accident while working on the Nauvoo Temple. In his remarks, Smith both elaborated the metaphysical foundations of the new theology and defended his prophetic status before the conference.[33] Smith's charisma and persuasive powers were never greater: the following day, the conference gave Smith what amounted to a clear vote of confidence by "sustaining" him as a candidate for the presidency of the United States.

Shortly following this conference, the chief figures in the dissent movement, including Law and Marks, were summarily cashiered from their ecclesiastical offices and excommunicated. The disaffected Mormons in Nauvoo continued their protests, however, and William Law acquired a press to publish a newspaper—the *Expositor*—that attacked Smith and publicized his perceived heresies to the outside world. As both mayor of Nauvoo and lieutenant general of the Nauvoo Legion, and possibly emboldened by the show of support at the April conference, Smith ordered a contingent of the Legion to destroy the opposition press as a public nuisance. The consequences of this rash action proved disastrous. To outsiders, the Mormons at Nauvoo seemed to have become a law unto themselves, acting with apparent legal impunity and dispensing their own justice. They would have to be stopped, their enemies raged, before they gained total domination of the region.

Vigilante mobs threatened to march on Nauvoo, and the governor of Illinois, now Thomas Ford, commanded the prophet's arrest on charges of riot. Smith considered fleeing the state, as he had done in Ohio and Missouri, but—after agonizingly contradictory advice from close family and friends—eventually surrendered to civil authorities and was taken to the county seat at Carthage to stand trial. There, on June 27, 1844, the life of the thirty-eight-year-old Mormon prophet was abruptly ended by a mob of assassins who stormed the jail in a barrage of bullets, killing both Joseph and his brother Hyrum, who ostensibly were lodged in custody for their own protection.

The Mormons at Nauvoo and nearby areas were stunned. Joseph had providentially escaped so many other threats, but now he was gone. As Brigham Roberts describes it, "His death had not been realistically contemplated by the body of the people. . . . Now that this calamity had befallen them, the Saints for the moment were as sheep without a shepherd."[34] After a period of mourning, struggle for control of the church predictably ensued. A special conference was held in Nauvoo in early August to resolve confusion and determine the future leadership and continuity of the restored church. At this conference the Twelve Apostles, with Brigham Young at their head, won the confidence of a majority of the people, while the leadership aspirations of Sidney Rigdon and others were rejected.

Prior to Smith's assassination, the apostles as a body had increasingly become Smith's staunchest supporters. The decision of the conference in favor of Young and the apostles appears, therefore, to have been based on the premise that Smith's most radical teachings, including plural marriage, were to continue to be implemented and not abandoned or reformed. The apostles acted swiftly to consolidate their position and excommunicated Rigdon and others, including Joseph's younger brother, William, who questioned the apostles' right to authority. As a consequence, the legitimacy and functioning of the office of the presiding patriarch was also keenly at issue. At a general conference of the church in October 1845, the Quorum of the Twelve Apostles was collectively sustained as the acting First Presidency of the Church of Jesus Christ of Latter-day Saints. The office of church patriarch, however, remained vacant until 1849, when the Utah Mormons chose John Smith, Joseph Sr.'s brother, to assume the hereditary position.[35]

Meanwhile, enemies in surrounding communities had assumed that elimination of the two Smith brothers would lead to the dissolution of Mormonism as an organizational entity. But when Young and the apostles firmly asserted their institutional authority instead, pushing ahead with construction work on the impressive Nauvoo Temple and continuing other significant church-sponsored projects, overt hostilities recommenced. As in Missouri, rabid anti-Mormon elements were determined to eradicate from their state, once and for all, the perceived Mormon plague. Public threats were made, quasi-militia and vigilante groups assembled, and depredations inflicted against outlying Mormon farms and families. Young and other Mormon leaders recalled all too well their disastrous experience in Missouri. They perceived the ultimate futility of armed resistance against the implacable opposition of hate-filled neighbors, who, they assumed, would inevitably be backed by state force. They concluded that, in order to survive, the Mormon movement that began in America would have to separate itself from the boundaries of American society. They decided that their best option was to seek a sanctuary either somewhere in the sparsely inhabited regions of Texas, which at the time was a section of northern Mexico, or in Mexican California. Thus, throughout 1845, the Mormon leadership was preoccupied with two primary tasks: completion of the Nauvoo Temple (so that the faithful could receive their long-awaited temple endowments of spiritual power and blessing from on high) and preparation for a massive Mormon exodus.

The exodus from Nauvoo would entail a 1,200-mile trek on foot and by wagon from the banks of the Mississippi to the eastern edge of the Rocky Mountains, ending in the high desert valley of the Great Salt Lake, where the faithful were determined to pursue the dreams of Zion unmolested by enemies and mob violence.[36] Not all of the Nauvoo Mormons, however, rallied to the leadership decisions put forward by the Twelve Apostles. Plural marriage and authority issues had fractured the unanimity of the Latter-day Saint community. Many stayed behind, including Joseph's wife Emma and her children; Joseph's mother, Lucy; and his brother William, erstwhile patriarch to the church. They and others who rejected the apostles' authority were to become the nucleus for what was called "the reorganization movement," once Joseph III attained his majority and agreed to assume the presidency of the Reorganized Church of Jesus Christ of Latter Day Saints (RLDS) in 1860.

Nonetheless, a majority of the Nauvoo Latter-day Saints again, as in past perilous times, disposed of their property and turned their faces west in preparation for an arduous march across the Great Plains, once more in search of Zion. The Latter-day Saint hegira from Nauvoo to the protecting bulwark of the Rocky Mountains has become a part of the legendary history of the American West. On their epic trek, Mormon refugees consciously identified with and emulated the children of Israel, submitting to the stern direction of Brigham Young, an American Moses, who guided them as God's covenant people through the wilderness in search of the promised land of their inheritance. To lift their spirits as they journeyed, Joseph Smith's stalwart scribe, William Clayton,[37] composed lyrics to the melody of an old English folk song, which was quickly adopted and sung along the trail by successive groups of Mormon immigrants:

Come, come, ye saints, no toil nor labor fear;
But with joy wend your way.
Though hard to you this journey may appear,
Grace shall be as your day.
'Tis better far for us to strive our useless cares from us to drive;
Do this, and joy your hearts will swell—
All is well! All is well!

Why should we mourn or think our lot is hard?
'Tis not so; all is right.
Why should we think to earn a great reward if we now shun the
     fight?
Gird up your loins; fresh courage take.
Our God will never us forsake;
And soon we'll have this tale to tell—
All is well! All is well!

We'll find the place which God for us prepared,
Far away, in the West,
Where none shall come to hurt or make afraid;
There the saints, will be blessed.
We'll make the air, with music ring,
Shout praises to our God and King;
Above the rest these words we'll tell—
All is well! All is well!

And should we die before our journey's through,
Happy day! All is well!
We then are free from toil and sorrow, too;
With the just we shall dwell!
But if our lives are spared again to see the Saints their rest obtain,
Oh, how we'll make this chorus swell—
All is well! All is well![38]

It was in the arid basin of the Wasatch Front that the Latter-day Saints
at long last found an enduring home. From the day Brigham Young and
the vanguard company of pioneers entered the isolated Salt Lake Valley
until the present time, Utah in general, and Salt Lake City in particular,
has been referred to by Latter-day Saints worldwide as Zion, the headquarters of their church and the nominal heartland of the Mormon people.

POSTSCRIPT: ON THE HISTORICAL CONTAINMENT
OF LDS ORACULAR PROPHECY

In our summary of the spiritual peregrinations of the early Latter-day Saints in search of salvation both on earth and in heaven, we have attempted to highlight those aspects of their history that demonstrate the simultaneously unifying and polarizing consequences of oracular new religions. In doing so, we have paid little attention to the actual chronology of Joseph Smith's published revelations accepted as scripture by the LDS Church and the complex interactive ways in which they were produced. In cursory review of his revelatory record, we recall for readers that Joseph Smith initiated his prophetic career with astonishing claims of a miraculous translation of the Book of Mormon, followed by contemporary oracular announcements. For several years thereafter his leadership relied heavily on oracular messages, peaking in 1831–32 with a total of twenty-seven revelations recorded in the LDS Church Doctrine and Covenants. These were revelations which Smith regularly offered as authentication of his prophetic status and divine justification for the emerging doctrines and organizational development of the LDS Church.

Smith's resort to official oracular prophecies tapered off in later years, however, as indicated by the chronology of revelations published in the Doctrine and Covenants: from a total of forty-seven in the first four years following the organization of the LDS Church in 1830 to only eight in the last four years of Smith's life (1840–44). During this latter period, especially in Nauvoo, Smith's confidence in his own leadership voice appeared to grow, as he increasingly relied on letters, organizational talks, and public sermons rather than dictating oracular prophecies as the means for directing his followers. Interestingly, however, when he formulated radically new doctrines during the latter years of his life (such as temple ordinances for proxy baptism of the dead in 1841 and plural marriage in 1843), they were accompanied by the dictation of strong oracular revelations.

Since Joseph Smith's death, only five statements under the imprimatur of succeeding prophet-presidents have been added as official texts to the Utah-based LDS Church's version of the Doctrine and Covenants. These are dated as being issued in 1844, 1847, 1890, 1918, and 1978. The first was in the form of an account of the assassination of Joseph Smith in 1844 and a memorialization of his prophetic calling by Apostle John Taylor (eventually third president of the LDS Church). This was followed in 1847 by Brigham Young's admonitory instructions to the Latter-day Saints as

"The word and will of the Lord concerning the Camp of Israel in their journeyings to the West," prior to the commencement of the Mormons' historic migration to the valley of the Great Salt Lake. Two major policy declarations subsequently have also been included in the LDS Doctrine and Covenants: President Wilford Woodruff's 1890 "manifesto," announcing the withdrawal of official church sanction for the practice of plural marriage, and President Spencer Kimball's 1978 announcement lifting the ban against males of African descent from being ordained to the LDS lay priesthood. All of these official additions to the Doctrine and Covenants are considered by contemporary Latter-day Saints to be inspired statements, but none are recorded in the language of oracular revelation. The only visionary, ultra-supernatural addition to the LDS canon was President Joseph F. Smith's (Hyrum Smith's son, born in Far West, Missouri) revelation in 1918 regarding the preaching of the restored gospel to departed spirits awaiting their chance to attain salvation in the afterlife.

The organization of the RLDS Church (subsequently renamed the Community of Christ) in 1860, with Joseph Smith Jr.'s oldest surviving son at the helm, also continued the practice of adding new revelations to their version of the Doctrine and Covenants. A systematic study and comparison of the official revelations of the LDS Church and Community of Christ since the death of their mutual founder would be an instructive undertaking for better understanding the generational endurance and development of new religions originating in oracular prophecy. While neither church has continued publishing nineteenth-century-style oracular revelations, the Community of Christ, by deemphasizing its distinctive prophetic origins and LDS doctrinal innovations, has moved much further in the direction of mainstream Christian assimilation than has the conservative, Utah-headquartered Church of Jesus Christ of Latter-day Saints.

THE OFFICE AND CALLING OF THE CHURCH PATRIARCH

Congruent with its restorationist ideology, covenantal priesthood identification with ancient Israel, and primal belief in contemporary revelation, one of the most interesting doctrinal practices to emerge in early Mormonism was the institutionalization of patriarchal blessings. According to Richard Bushman, "The office [of the patriarch] emerged out of the practice of public blessings administered by Joseph and by various fathers, most notably Joseph's own father, Joseph Smith Sr. Gradually these spontaneous blessings evolved into more systematic blessings of comfort and direction and were regularized in the office of the patriarch."[1] As succinctly stated by Irene Bates and Gary Smith, "Beginning with Joseph Sr.'s tenure, and largely defined by it, the hereditary calling of the Patriarch in the LDS Church was modeled on the Old Testament patriarchs."[2]

Eligible blessing recipients included all faithful members of the church, both male and female. Large numbers of Latter-day Saints eagerly sought their blessings from the patriarch, once instituted. We have argued that the supernatural valence consequently attached to these blessings and their doctrinal substance sustained and strengthened members' religious conviction, thereby supporting the propagation of Mormonism as a new religion. In the following chapters we fortify this thesis by first reviewing the patriarch's inaugural prophetic status and ministry among the Kirtland Latter-day Saints. We then summarize in chapter 4 our methodology for reviewing and analyzing the contents of a substantial number of early blessings bestowed between 1834 and 1845. In chapter 5, we identify and describe the most salient doctrinal themes contained in those blessings.

And in chapter 6 we systematically compare the blessings of male and female converts to early Mormonism. Taken as a whole, our findings illuminate the distinctive manner in which patriarchal blessings both expressed and reinforced the doctrinal faith and religious aspirations of Mormonism's founding generation.

ORIGIN OF THE OFFICE OF CHURCH PATRIARCH

In December 1833 or 1834, Joseph Smith ordained his father, Joseph Smith Sr., as patriarch (officially designated thereafter as Patriarch to the Church or Presiding Patriarch).[3] If the 1833 date is correct, the ordination of Father Smith as patriarch occurred as part of a dedication ceremony of a new press in Kirtland for publishing the *Evening and Morning Star*, the first Mormon newspaper. (A Missouri mob had destroyed the original church press in July of that year.) As Bates and Smith describe the occasion, "To the participants, this was a historic moment. It represented victory over the enemies of the church in a significant arena, and the celebratory spirit manifested itself in blessings bestowed by the Prophet on his family and friends assembled there." Bates and Smith go on to point out that "whether Joseph knew in advance he was going to create an office in the church before he began to speak to his father in blessing is not known." Furthermore, while Father Smith was blessed with "the keys of the patriarchal priesthood over the kingdom of God on earth," in his ordination blessing there "was no explanation of the responsibilities that attended holding the keys of the patriarchal priesthood." Nonetheless, "it was soon implicitly accepted that [Father Smith's] calling included the right to bestow blessings on all members of the church, as well as to preside over any other patriarchs who would be called on a local basis."[4]

It also was understood that, as a restored priesthood office of ancient Hebraic origins, the patriarchate devolved on Father Smith and his male descendants after him by right of primogeniture. Thus, upon Father Smith's death in 1840, his oldest living son, Hyrum, assumed the hereditary office of church patriarch. Subsequently, following Hyrum's untimely assassination alongside the prophet Joseph in 1844, their younger brother William's claim of hereditary succession to the office of church patriarch was initially recognized by Brigham Young and the Quorum of the Twelve Apostles.[5]

As mentioned in the introduction, Richard Bushman advances the theory that the office of the patriarch was created by Joseph Smith Jr. through revelation in conjunction with his sympathetic loyalty and support for his aging father, "the feelings of a son for a father who had suffered repeated defeats":

> This was a man who had lost one farm when his storekeeping business failed, who had been reduced to tenancy for fourteen years while his children were young, and then lost a second farm when he missed the mortgage payments. Fifty-eight years old when the Church was organized, Joseph Sr. was back in tenancy, with no house or land to call his own. Defeated by the rigors of the economic order, he was told by his son he would be a prince over his posterity. "Blessed of the Lord is my father," Joseph said, "for he shall stand in the midst of his posterity and shall be comforted by their blessings when he is old and bowed down with years, and he shall be called a prince over them." Like Adam, he would assemble his children—his one undoubted accomplishment—and "sit in the general assembly of patriarchs, even in council with the Ancient of Days when he shall sit and all the patriarchs with him—and shall enjoy his right and authority under the Ancient of Days." . . .
>
> Joseph Sr. seemed to understand that his sons had redeemed his life. When he blessed Joseph and Hyrum in December 1834, he thanked them for enduring the hardships of their early lives. . . .
>
> . . . Now, at last, the father could bless his son "with the blessings of thy fathers Abraham, Isaac and Jacob." Joseph Sr. had given his son nothing for a worldly inheritance, and Joseph Jr. had met this lack by giving his father the power to bless his sons.[6]

Thus, among other things, patriarchal blessings were considered to be a special type of father's blessing to his children. In his subsequent blessings of the Latter-day Saints, Father Smith would often address those recipients whose parents had rejected or not joined the Mormon Church as "orphans," for whom he assumed a vicarious responsibility to bless in the name of the Lord. The following examples are typical.

Blessing of Charles Jameson, March 21, 1836: "I lay my hands upon thy head in the name of the Lord and seal a father's blessing upon thee, for thou art an orphan and hast no father to bless thee, but God shall be thy father, and he hath reserved a blessing for thee."[7]

Blessing of Lyman Leonard, May 2, 1836: "I lay my hands upon thy head and bless thee in the name of the Lord with a father's blessing. Thou art entitled to a father's blessing because thou art an orphan, that thou mayest receive an inheritance among thy brethren, and be equal to them in all things."[8]

Blessing of Desdamona Fulmer, February 9, 1837: "I lay my hands on thy head in the room of a father to bless thee, for thou standest as an orphan to me. I say thou shalt have the desires of thy heart for thy father's family."[9]

Blessing of Sophia Packard, December 13, 1837: "[I] bless thee with the blessing of a Father. Thou hast a father yet he cannot bless thee because he does not stand in the authority of the holy priesthood. The most of thy kindred flesh consider thee to be a cast away, but I say unto thee, thou art not a cast away, for thou dost belong to the household of faith."[10]

While Mormon fathers who were ordained to the lay priesthood retained the right to give spontaneous blessings to their own children and other family members—particularly blessings of restored health when their loved ones fell ill—the emergent practice of fathers bestowing patriarchal blessings to their children yielded to the institutional norm of every worthy Latter-day Saint receiving his or her official patriarchal blessing under the hands of the presiding patriarch, who was ceded the right to issue such blessings by virtue of the restored authority of his office.

THE COMPENSATORY RITUAL CHARACTER
OF EARLY PATRIARCHAL BLESSINGS

Institutionalized group rituals (as opposed to personal rituals) are formally authorized, scripted actions that typically display the characteristics of a performance.[11] As performance, rituals involve authorized actors who, through prescribed speech, symbolic gestures, and scripted actions, aim to stimulate and shape the feelings of an audience. Religious studies scholar Aldo Terrin defines ritual as "formal and symbolic behavior that leads to the creation or recreation of an emotion in order to obtain or maintain a correct balance between persons and the world."[12] In religious communities, rituals are performed in a variety of contexts and are focused on a wide range of particular group objectives correlated with the community's core beliefs and ultimate concerns. Worship rites and sacraments supplemented by numerous rites of passage ceremonies (including marriage and funeral rites), atonement and purification rites, ordinations to office, oaths of allegiance, and various dedication ceremonies are but a few examples of rituals commonly performed in religious communities.

Students of ritual are divided in their views as to what aspects of ritual performance should receive priority attention, the principal alternatives being the particular form rituals take (their scripted gestures and sequential actions, including chanting, singing, rhythmic movements, and so on) or their ideational contents (the manifest and/or latent meanings of what is said or symbolized).[13] The stimulation and renewal of feelings of reverence, joy, ecstasy, gratitude, responsibility, unity, devotion, and "spiritual enlightenment" that reinforce group commitment and mutual identification are salient products of ritual participation by community members. Is it primarily the physical form or the ideational content of ritual performances that stimulates and shapes participants' feelings in these ways? The conceptual categories of form and content are not, of course, mutually exclusive in the process of striking "a correct balance between persons and the world." At the same time, it is plausible to assume that the relative importance of these two aspects of ritual performance may shift and vary from one ritual context to another.

In the case of LDS patriarchal blessings, the ideational content of the blessing clearly predominates. The scripted form of patriarchal blessings is simplicity itself. The patriarch lays both of his hands on the blessing recipient's head and leaves them there until his benediction is complete. The patriarch wears no special garment or regalia to set him apart from the recipient or other onlookers, nor does he conspicuously display or manipulate religious props or sacred symbols. The acknowledged authority of his office—and the shared belief that through that authority he receives and communicates God's blessing and intentions for recipients— bestows upon the patriarch a revered religious status in the Latter-day Saint community.

In the performance of his role, then, the patriarch himself is a symbol of God's beneficence. The one symbolic gesture he employs in bestowing blessings is the laying on of hands, which signifies God's will and power channeled directly through the patriarch to the blessing recipient. There is no rigidly prescribed wording that the patriarch must use in all blessings he bestows, but a simple format is routinely followed. The patriarch begins with an invocation in which he addresses the recipient by name and announces that the blessing is being issued in the name of a deity (usually referencing Jesus Christ). At the blessing's end, the patriarch also commonly "seals" his benediction in Christ's name. This latter pronouncement is of paramount significance to Latter-day Saints, signifying as it does a binding and eternal promise in the sight of God.[14] Between the invocation and the benediction, the patriarch is at liberty to express whatever communicative content he feels inspired to offer. Thus there is an extemporaneous quality in patriarchal blessings that permits the patriarch to personalize his words to each individual recipient.[15] Because they are regarded by recipients to be inspired utterances, the patriarch's words are accorded the utmost importance. Their present meanings and future portents are eagerly scrutinized and typically reflected upon as a meaningful guide throughout one's life.[16]

While the substantive content of the blessing may occasionally induce tears of joy, the LDS response to performance gestures normally involves reverential concentration on the meaning of the patriarch's words, not ecstatic expressions. At the same time, many early patriarchal blessings demonstrate common ideational themes that, as we will demonstrate in chapters 5 and 6, can only be fully appreciated within the context of early Mormonism's doctrinal development. For LDS converts, belief in the latter-day restoration through the agency of a living prophet and the delegated priesthood authority of the patriarch to pronounce God's word and will to the people in blessing was the primary source of enhanced feelings of gratitude and rejoicing upon receipt of their personal blessings.

Patriarchal blessings projected the early Latter-day Saints as God's chosen servants in the last days and confirmed their transcendent destiny to participate in the realization of the divine plan of human salvation—their many trials and ordeals notwithstanding. The blessings thus produced shared feelings of a "correct balance" between Mormon adherents and the world. Embattled new religions, such as nineteenth-century Mormonism, must struggle with the discrepancy between their members' sense of divine mission and special favor in the sight of God and their denigrated, marginal standing in the world. Their material hardships and social marginalization must somehow be compensated by faith in an ultimate reward and shared triumph. Themes of ultimate compensation and triumph were, in fact, major motifs in early patriarchal blessings, as demonstrated by our statistical content analysis of these blessings (summarized in the succeeding chapters). In part we may thus describe early patriarchal blessings as *compensatory* commitment rituals.[17] Their compensatory functions were further enhanced by the fact that they were not only pronounced orally but also recorded by a scribe. Written copies subsequently were given to blessing recipients to treasure in their possession as sacred documents; recipients would ponder them, be guided by them, and even pass them on to their children as tangible testimonials of God's power and beneficence through the restored priesthood medium of his chosen servants.[18]

THE COMMUNAL CHARACTER OF
EARLY PATRIARCHAL BLESSINGS

Shared feelings evoked through the enactment of ritual performances serve to renew and strengthen the bonds that unite members of a community. This is particularly true when rituals are performed in social settings in which like-minded individuals, who already share core values and beliefs, are assembled together. In his newly ordained capacity as presiding patriarch to the church, the blessings Father Smith began bestowing on Mormon converts in Kirtland, Ohio, were, in Lavina Fielding Anderson's words, "quasi-public affairs."[19] Blessing meetings in Kirtland initially were conducted in people's homes, with family members as well as other LDS neighbors typically present. At these meetings, multiple individuals would often be blessed in sequence, accompanied by group prayer and hymn singing. The ritual function of producing feelings of community solidarity and shared commitment was undoubtedly amplified when patriarchal blessings were publicly issued in these kinds of group settings.

Blessing meetings were also occasionally combined with "feast" meetings. Mark Staker's account of the early development of LDS church doctrine and organization in Kirtland, for example, notes that a "pattern developed that combined meetings at which members received patriarchal blessings from Joseph Smith Sr. with a dinner 'for the poor.'" Staker goes on to quote an early convert in Kirtland, Ira Ames, as saying on March 13, 1834, "I received my Patriarchal Blessing under the hands of Joseph Smith Senior at a feast and blessing meeting which I made at my house for the widows and orphans. . . . [I]t was a very pleasant time, a glorious meeting." Similarly, Staker writes that early Kirtland stalwarts "N. K. and Ann [Whitney] hosted the blessing meeting and feast at which Samuel and Susanna

Whitney received their patriarchal blessings along with other individuals. It was a special event, three days of celebrations the likes of which had never before been seen in Kirtland." Staker also quotes Ann Whitney saying of this occasion, "According to our Savior's pattern and agreeably to the Prophet Joseph's and our own ideas of true charity and disinterested benevolence, we determined to make a feast for the poor, such as we knew could not return the same to us; the lame, the halt; the deaf; the blind; the aged and infirm."[20]

Patriarchal blessings given in conjunction with "feast meetings for the poor" further served to reinforce members' feelings of mutual identification and commitment to the egalitarian ideals of Zion. Once the Kirtland Temple was dedicated in 1836, blessing meetings were conducted in the temple assembly hall where Father Smith sometimes presided over meetings of the Kirtland High Council.[21] Like religious gatherings in general, blessing meetings served an important community function in which church members' commitments were publicly reiterated and mutually reinforced. As Anderson points out, the sacred character (or supernatural valence) attached to patriarchal blessings undoubtedly was enhanced even more strongly when pronounced in the temple, which itself had been ritually dedicated for the purpose of conducting God's work on earth.[22] In contrast, today's LDS patriarchal blessings are routinely issued to individual members in private rather than public settings. (We will return later to this significant change of the standard social setting for patriarchal blessings.)

Anderson also remarks on Father Smith's bolstered status at communal blessing meetings as church patriarch and the corresponding prayerful sincerity with which he issued blessings to the faithful. She includes several illustrative examples: "As a prelude to blessing the forty-two-year old Jemima Johnson," for instance, "the venerable sixty-five-old Joseph said, 'I pray to show me by his vision his will and his blessing for thee. I want to speak to thee just as God would speak should he now lay his hands on thy head to bless thee.'"[23] Similarly, in another blessing the patriarch said, "Sister [Rebecca] Williams, in the name of Jesus Christ of Nazareth I lay my hands upon thy head, and I ask my heavenly Father to put words and thoughts into my heart, and also, to prepare thee for a blessing."[24] At another time, he prayed, "Sister Mary [Baldwin], In the name of Jesus Christ I pray God the Father, that thou mayest be as Mary at the feet of Jesus that thou mayest be blessed with the ministry of angels."[25] On behalf of Lorenzo Snow, the patriarch prayed, "I ask God the Eternal Father, who has called me to the office of the priesthood, to open the visions of my mind and give me the Holy Spirit."[26] Such petitions expressed and reinforced the revelatory premise shared by the patriarch and his blessing recipients that the veil separating heaven and earth had been made permeable through the agency of God's latter-day oracles, reemphasizing to believers the charismatic authority invested in the office of the patriarch.

Patriarchal blessings were authoritatively pronounced, using first-person biblical language as though God, through the agency of the patriarch, was speaking directly and personally to each blessing recipient. The patriarchs' blessings employed prophetic rhetoric similar to the oracular language modeled by Joseph Smith Jr. in his published revelations on church government and doctrine. While these blessings were limited to individual cases and did not establish official doctrine or church policy, patriarchal blessings administered to believing Latter-day Saints were nevertheless charged with supernatural valence. Like the prophet Joseph, the Smith patriarchs were believed to have revelatory power as authoritative conduits of God's grace and inspiration for his covenant people (though their pronouncements were comparatively circumscribed in scope and organizational impact). Sociologically, we can appreciate how these early blessings served as a powerful compensatory mechanism for reinforcing converts' solidarity and commitment to their new religion and to their leaders' priesthood authority in the face of sustained adversity. They were taken very seriously by early converts, who felt privileged to be blessed by Joseph Sr.—revered as the father of God's latter-day prophet—and later, in succession, by the prophet's brothers Hyrum and William when they, in turn, assumed the hereditary mantle of church patriarch.[27]

In discussing the communal character of early patriarchal blessings, it should also be mentioned that patriarchs, beginning with Joseph Sr., were remunerated financially (as were their scribes and recorders) for the blessings they issued.[28] This anomalous practice—Latter-day Saints have always prided themselves on sustaining an unpaid lay clergy—was halted in 1914, and patriarchal blessings have since been given gratis to individuals who seek them in faith and humility and are deemed worthy.[29] In any event, the modest cost of early patriarchal blessings did not dampen members' anxious desire to obtain them, nor were pecuniary motives commonly imputed by cynics to the Smith patriarchs' exercise of their office.

HEBRAIC LINKS: PATRIARCHAL BLESSINGS
AND COVENANTAL PRIESTHOOD LINEAGE

As we have emphasized, the extemporaneous words pronounced in patriarchal blessings were received with heartfelt gratitude. They were considered to be the inspired word of God, addressed directly and personally to individual blessing recipients and, in conformity with the ideology of the restoration, they constituted an important form of prophetic revelation. The LDS notion of restoration, however, includes far more than a renewal of prophetic communication with God, reaching back, as it does, to incorporate theological and ritual elements from the Hebraic origins of Christianity. LDS patriarchal blessings were modeled on the Old Testament account of Israel blessing his sons. The institution of the office of church patriarch and the priesthood sealing authority of his blessings were important elements in the expanding Mormon comprehension of the latter-day restoration, which included the Mormons' literal kinship with the ancient Hebrews as God's covenant people. Thus, in conjunction with his bestowal of personal blessing, the church patriarch typically traced blessing recipients' lineages as descending from one of the Twelve Tribes of Israel. Increasing Mormon emphasis on lineal descent and identification with ancient Israel appears, at least in part, to have arisen from Joseph Smith's preoccupation with the issue of religious authority—an issue that underlay the justification of virtually every LDS doctrinal and organizational innovation. The creative amalgamation of Old Testament and New Testament religious claims in the Mormon restoration supports Jan Shipps's influential thesis that Mormonism is not merely another Christian sect but constitutes a new religious tradition in the world religious economy.[30]

According to D. Michael Quinn, the practice of prophetically confirming Latter-day Saints' Hebraic lineage through patriarchal blessings institutionalized a nascent "tribalism" that had already been developing in early Mormonism, resulting in the formation of sharp moral boundaries separating Mormons from non-Mormons.[31] Congruent with Quinn's analysis is Shipps's argument that the overlay of a strong Hebraic dimension to Mormonism's Christian restorationist claims ultimately "would carry the Saints beyond the metaphorical Christian understanding of adoption into Israel to a conviction that the actual blood of Israel coursed through their veins. For the Mormons, this conviction separated humanity into two camps: those who were members of Abraham's family and those who were not. The former (Latter-day Saints and Jews) were God's chosen people;

all the rest were Gentile."[32] Moreover, Shipps notes, in conjunction with the development of temple rituals (including celestial marriage) and the associated doctrines of deification, Mormonism's identification with ancient Israel shifted public perception of the early Latter-day Saints: to outsiders, they were not merely another contentious Christian sect, but an altogether alien entity.

In heretical contrast to the priesthood doctrines of most New Testament Christians, Joseph Smith argued for a continuation of priesthood authority from the beginning of the Old Testament era to the present day. The priesthood of God, as envisioned in the Book of Mormon and specified in some of Joseph Smith's earliest revelations, was viewed as eternal. Smith and subsequent Mormon theologians maintained that various orders of the priesthood (Melchizedek and Aaronic) were never abrogated, discontinued, or supplanted by a "new priesthood" with the advent of New Testament Christianity.[33] According to Mormon doctrine, the eternal priesthood first entrusted to the ancient Hebrew patriarchs and later transmitted by Jesus to his disciples had to be *restored directly*—that is to say, literally passed on by those who previously possessed it. In the narrative claims of Mormon ecclesiology, both the Aaronic and Melchizedek priesthoods were restored through the laying on of hands by John the Baptist and the apostles Peter, James, and John, respectively, who ostensibly appeared to Joseph Smith and Oliver Cowdery sometime in 1829 as celestialized beings to delegate to them the authority to restore Christ's church.[34] Here we see a prime example of the kind of supernatural literalism that appealed so strongly to early Mormon converts. To them, accounts of ministering angels, heavenly messengers, and departed spirit agents clinched rather than diluted their enthusiastic acceptance of the restored gospel as proclaimed by Joseph Smith.

As they came to understand Smith's revelations, the restored priesthood signified divine authority *and* a covenantal relationship with the God of both the Old and New Testaments. In line with the Calvinistic theology of their New England ancestors, Mormons construed themselves as a "covenant people," both collectively and individually. The notion of sacred covenants between God and his children—in which the deity proffers blessings in exchange for solemn promises to obey his laws—informs virtually every aspect of LDS doctrine and corresponding religious practices. Mormons contend that God's proffered covenants, and the proper ritual means by which they are to be symbolically enacted (as in baptism or marriage), must come through revelation and the authority of the restored priesthood.[35] Thus, belief in the literal restoration of the priesthood through the supernatural intervention of agents from the spirit world not only meant that Mormon converts were properly authorized to act in God's name, but also signified to them that they were covenantal heirs of God's promises to the children of Abraham, Isaac, and Jacob. And in particular, through the lineage of Jacob's favored son, Joseph, they were proclaimed heirs of the promises to the Tribes of Ephraim and Manasseh, who formed the House of Joseph. Quite literally, in fact, early Mormons believed that they were descended from the fabled "Ten Lost Tribes" of Israel, whose members were presumed to have dispersed throughout the world dating from the Babylonian Captivity in 721 B.C. (hence the designation of one's lineage given in patriarchal blessings to recipients). A major impetus of Mormon proselytizing has been, from its beginning, to gather Israelite descendants from among the nations and reunite them as a people to build up Zion and receive, at long last, their promised blessings in the latter days of human history.[36]

In doctrinal tandem with the institutionalization of patriarchal blessings, therefore, was the LDS elaboration of Christian restoration theology, which very quickly went beyond mere revival of spiritual gifts and the New Testament apostolic church. What increasingly set the Latter-day Saints apart theologically from other restorationist groups was their insistence that, through the restored priesthood, God had authorized Joseph Smith to usher in what they believed was the "last dispensation of the fullness of times." The last dispensation was designated as the end time or the latter days of human history, in which the "fullness" of God's plan of salvation would be revealed as part of the "restoration of all things."[37] The restoration of all things significantly included Old Testament covenants and institutions, such as patriarchal priesthood authority, prophetic guidance, temple worship, and—most controversially—plural marriage, as well as the promise of an inheritance in Zion, where God would dwell with his covenant people.[38] These distinctively Mormon restorationist claims dovetailed with the emerging "sealing" ceremonies performed in LDS temples and the corresponding doctrines of "exaltation" and eternal life in God's celestial kingdom.[39]

In oracular voice and approaching the end of his meteoric life, Joseph Smith Jr. expounded on the sealing power of the restored priesthood and the "keys" of this power, which made delegation of authority in the church possible (including, by inference, the patriarch's authority to bless the people):

All covenants, contracts, bonds, obligations, oaths, vows, performances, connections, associations, or expectations, that are not made
and entered into and sealed by the Holy Spirit of promise, of him
who is anointed, both as well for time and all eternity, and that too
most holy, by revelation and commandment through the medium of
mine anointed, whom I have appointed on the earth to hold this
power . . . are of no efficacy, virtue, or force in and after the resurrection of the dead; for all contracts that are not made unto this end
have an end when men are dead.[40]

The purported sealing power of the restored priesthood and the delegated
"keys" to its exercise have become the central doctrines that, in conjunction with fundamental belief in contemporary revelation, bind the faith
and commitment of Latter-day Saints in compliance with the directives of
both their local congregational leaders and the general authorities of the
LDS Church.

EXCERPTS FROM EARLY PATRIARCHAL BLESSINGS
ILLUSTRATING PROPHETIC COMMITMENT LANGUAGE

To further illustrate the prophetic mode of language and some of the
doctrinal themes commonly contained in early LDS blessings, we have
selected and excerpted portions of blessings issued by Joseph Smith Sr.,
Hyrum, and William in the years 1834 through 1845. Like the prophet
himself, all three Smith patriarchs demonstrated impressive, extemporaneous language skills for rural laymen, untutored in the dialectics of the
trained clergy. Through the delegated sealing power of their patriarchal
office, their compensatory blessings were considered to be efficacious both
on earth and in heaven, for time and eternity.

The following excerpt is from the patriarchal blessing of Charles C.
Rich, pronounced by Joseph Smith Sr. on April 2, 1836, in Kirtland,
Ohio.[41]

Brother Charles, in the name of Jesus Christ of Nazareth, I lay my
hands upon thy head and seal blessings according to the power of
the holy priesthood. . . . Thou art a Son of Zion and have been willing
to lay down thy life for thy brethren. . . . Thou art a son of Joseph,
an Ephraimite by blood. The Lord hath looked on thee from the

beginning and chosen thee from the foundation of the world to be a polished shaft in his quiver. . . . thy name is sealed in heaven, never to be blotted out . . . Satan shall have no power over thee . . . the Lord is thy deliverer, and thy life is hid with Christ in God and shall be kept from the destroyer . . . thou shalt preach the gospel till the Savior comes in the clouds of heaven. . . . Thy posterity shall be blessed after thee and thy blessing shall reach unto thy children . . . and they shall reign with thee in the kingdom of heaven on earth, for thou art one of the hundred and forty and four thousand, which will stand upon Mount Zion with white robes. . . . Thou shalt gather thousands to Zion. . . . Thou shalt weep over them when thou seest their calamities and seek them out and send them up to Zion. . . . Thou shalt be a blessing to all wherever you shall go . . . and thou shalt have all the power of the holy priesthood. . . . These blessings I seal for thee in the name of Jesus.

This excerpt is from the patriarchal blessing of Susanna White, pronounced by Hyrum Smith on September 8, 1841, in Nauvoo, Illinois.[42]

Susanna, I lay my hands upon your head, in the name of Jesus of Nazareth, to bless you . . . for your benefit and the benefit of your posterity and kinsfolk, that you might have a name in Israel, as a daughter of Abraham in the lineage of Joseph . . . and as a mother in Israel . . . to receive the honor of that blessing in the fullness of time. . . . I seal upon your head the gift of eternal life . . . in connection with one who holdeth the keys for the knowledge of God . . . even the fullness of the revelations of Jesus Christ in these last days. . . . The Lord has looked upon your integrity . . . and called you from your native country, from your kinfolk, in answer to the prayers of your fathers. . . . Notwithstanding . . . tribulation awaits you, trials, sorrowing. In them you shall be sustained and supported by the grace of God in the hour of your deepest affliction . . . the truth of these promises shall have this sign . . . another Comforter, that when you read these lines you will feel glad in your heart, which Comforter is the promise of eternal life. Your children shall have the priesthood and their names shall be honored in the midst of the princes of Israel . . . your years shall be many and you shall receive an inheritance in time and eternity.

The last excerpt is from the patriarchal blessing of Levi Runyan, pronounced by William Smith on July 30, 1845, in Nauvoo, Illinois.[43]

> Beloved brother, I lay my hands upon your head in the name of the
> Lord Jesus Christ . . . the priesthood after the holy order with all the
> powers and privileges shall be sealed upon thy head, with appoint-
> ments and ordinations greater than thou hast yet received . . . even
> that exaltation that belongs to the servants of the most high God . . .
> the Holy Spirit shall be given unto thee . . . the heavens shall be
> opened. Angels shall be sent to administer unto thee, and by visions
> and dreams the will of God shall be unfolded. . . . Unto thee is
> appointed to a great work . . . enemies may deride thee and scoff . . .
> yet thy courage shall increase . . . and by wisdom that cometh from
> on high none can resist the power of thy testimony . . . these are the
> days of tribulation, the time of wars and rumors of war . . . thou shalt
> rise up like Melchisedec of old to establish peace in the land and
> gather out the lost sheep of the house of Israel . . . thou shalt see
> Zion go forth . . . and all who battle against it shall be brought to
> naught . . . and *if thou art faithful* [italics added] . . . thou shalt come
> up on Mount Zion as a Savior of many of your brethren who are of
> the seed of Joseph, whose blood thou art . . . this shall be thy minis-
> try, thy glory, thy power, and thy salvation, for I seal it upon thy head
> in the name of Jesus Christ.

While the general substance and form of early patriarchal blessings given
to thousands of blessing recipients seem repetitious, the blessings were
pronounced extemporaneously and therefore displayed a certain range of
idiosyncratic variation, as the above excerpts demonstrate. At the same
time, the overall thematic unity of these early blessings is also evident.
They were permeated with the religious hopes and aspirations of the Mormon restoration and employed phrasing and concepts that resonated with
and reinforced specific Mormon doctrines. In spite of their lack of formal
rhetorical training, all three Smith patriarchs had a fine command of
religious language in general and were even capable of eloquence in the
blessings they bestowed upon the Latter-day Saints. This, no doubt, was
additional evidence to blessing recipients that the words of the patriarchs
were inspired by God. The recipients accepted the ultimate veracity of their
blessings with humility and gratitude as a transcendent beacon of hope
and inspiration in their lives.

THE PROBLEMS AND PROMISE OF PATRIARCHAL
BLESSINGS AS HISTORICAL ARTIFACTS

As noted in the previous chapter, patriarchal blessings were not only pronounced verbally and extemporaneously but also recorded in writing, with
one copy going to the recipients and another kept as an official church
record of the blessing. Michael Marquardt succinctly summarizes this process: "The persons blessed usually retained the original handwritten blessing.
At a subsequent date, they would bring their blessing to a Church recorder
to be copied into the official blessing book."[1] The positions of blessing scribe
and/or clerk and recorder were considered to be church callings. As previously mentioned, in the early decades of the Mormon restoration, they,
along with the church patriarch, were paid fees for their services. In addition
to the substance of the blessings themselves, other information was also
typically added to the documentary record, including the date of the blessing;
where the blessing was given; the blessing recipient's full name and date
and place of birth; the name of the patriarch who bestowed the blessing; and
(usually) the name of the scribe, clerk, and/or recorder.

The first official "clerk and recorder" of patriarchal blessings was Oliver
Cowdery. Cowdery was arguably the best-qualified person at the time to
serve in that capacity. When Joseph Smith Jr. was bogged down in his initial
translation efforts to dictate the text of the Book of Mormon, it was Cowdery
who became his faithful scribe in April 1829. Within three intense months
of dictation and transcription, a handwritten manuscript copy of the 531-
page book was produced for publication. Cowdery acted in the unofficial
capacity of first LDS church historian and assumed responsibility for keeping a record of the church and its activities, including minutes of meetings

and patriarchal blessings. For many of Father Smith's earliest Kirtland blessings, Cowdery was listed as both clerk and recorder.[2] Over time (particularly after Cowdery became preoccupied with overseeing church publications in both Kirtland and Missouri), other men were designated either as clerks or scribes, whose job was to write down the words of the patriarch as though taking dictation, or as recorders, who then copied the scribe's transcription as a record for the church. In a survey of Marquardt's compilation of early patriarchal blessings, we counted a total of only two men (Oliver Cowdery and George W. Robinson) who were listed as both clerk and recorder. Sixteen different men were identified as clerks, and thirteen as scribes; only five were referred to as "recorders" between 1834 and 1845.[3]

LIMITATIONS OF PATRIARCHAL BLESSINGS AS HISTORICAL DOCUMENTS

As indicated, producing patriarchal blessings as written documents required scribes (or clerks) to be present when blessings were given in order to make a careful transcription of what was said, the original copy being given to the recipient and a second copy kept as an official document. The training, skill, and care with which this was done presumably varied from one scribe or recorder to another. Some words or parts of a blessing may inadvertently have been missed by the scribe in his notations and were therefore absent in the written record. In copying the scribe's transcription, recorders might inadvertently have made errors. Grammatical mistakes in the written copies of early blessings were not infrequent and may be attributed to errors in the patriarch's extemporaneous speech, the scribe's transcription, and/or the recorder's copied version of the blessing. (Spelling errors in written blessings can, of course, be attributed to the scribes and/or recorders alone.) In a few cases, some of the wording in officially recorded blessings was either modified or stricken from the record, and a few other blessings were recorded as summaries rather than verbatim transcriptions. Some blessings were not recorded for months or even years after they were pronounced.[4] Thus, early recorded blessings must be considered as more or less accurate facsimiles rather than perfect reproductions of every word or phrase as exactly spoken by patriarchs to their blessing recipients. (Today, LDS patriarchal blessings are sound-recorded when pronounced and subsequently transcribed into verbatim written copies.[5])

The fact that records of early LDS patriarchal blessings were made and preserved at all is a significant boon to historians. Even in the often hostile frontier environments of their early history, Mormons attached importance to careful record keeping. At the same time, the inexact recording of early patriarchal blessings creates reliability problems familiar to scholars of religious texts in other faith traditions.[6] The blessings' less-than-perfect reproduction is one limitation that scholars must take into account when using them as historical sources for inferring patterns of early doctrinal development and religious commitment among the Latter-day Saints. Other (and arguably bigger) problems for scholars involve the availability and accessibility of blessing documents. Though typically written down, many blessings were not preserved as official church records ("through the negligence of the scribes")[7] or were simply lost, as the Latter-day Saints endured numerous upheavals and periodically embarked on mass migrations under duress in trying and often primitive circumstances. The unknown quantity of missing documents from the historical record makes it difficult to determine how representative the recorded blessings are of the total number of blessings actually issued.

Furthermore, over time, the original public character of patriarchal blessings became increasingly privatized. As noted above, early patriarchal blessings were often bestowed as an aspect of Mormon community worship; family members and neighbors assembled in "blessing meetings," where all present could hear and rejoice in the prophetic pronouncements of the patriarch. As a form of community worship, patriarchal blessing meetings contributed significantly to the loyalty and solidarity of early Latter-day Saints' shared commitments to their religion. We cannot say with historical precision when blessing meetings ceased to be normative in Latter-day Saint communities. We surmise that the decline of this practice was a gradual process—that with the passage of time and increasing numbers of new converts, informal new norms developed without official guidelines being handed down to local patriarchs. While we lack documentation that would identify a particular time or formal rationale for this change, private appointments with the patriarch for the purpose of receiving a personal blessing have become the normative practice.

Along with this shift in the setting of patriarchal blessings emerged the belief that their contents were privileged information. Like the consultations and recommendations made by one's private doctor, attorney, or accountant, the contents of one's patriarchal blessing are no longer commonly publicized but shared only with one's family members. The increasing privatization of patriarchal blessings was historically congruent with the late nineteenth-century and twentieth-century ascendance of confidentiality norms generated through the proliferation of professional service occupations in the secular economy. LDS officials as well as ordinary church members have correspondingly become more protective of their patriarchal blessing documents. Today, public access to patriarchal blessings on file in the LDS archives is virtually closed. (With acceptable identification credentials, individuals can obtain copies of their own or family members' or relatives' blessings if they have been lost or are not in the individuals' personal possession). Generally speaking, the only way to see or get copies of other people's contemporary blessings for research purposes is to obtain permission from individuals who have personal copies in their possession and are willing to share them.

Problems of accuracy and accessibility notwithstanding, available patriarchal blessings are still a potential gold mine of information and insight into the religious culture of the Latter-day Saints. Verifiably accurate dates, correct names and locations of individuals identified in documents, and the specific wording attributed to particular sources can be of crucial importance to the ideographic concerns of genealogists, biographers, historians, archivists, literary critics, and document connoisseurs. For the nomothetic or generalizing concerns of social science, however, such individual case particulars are somewhat less important. If the specific dates or locations of particular blessings are occasionally in error, or if the contents of certain individual blessings do not record a patriarch's utterances perfectly accurately, when assembled in sufficient quantity, early patriarchal blessings still demonstrate similarities in both form and content. These meaningful cultural artifacts shed light on the foundational beliefs and aspirations of a successful new religious movement in the early years of its development and growth.

MARQUARDT'S COMPILATION OF
EARLY PATRIARCHAL BLESSINGS

In 1993 Irene Bates published a pioneering article on thematic changes in LDS patriarchal blessings from 1833 to 1979.[8] Bates reports that a substantial majority of nineteenth-century blessings in her sample were arduously obtained from personal journals or diaries, rather than published sources, and that virtually all of the twentieth-century blessings in her sample were obtained from individuals who voluntarily responded to her requests to share them for her research. Bates's research was much broader and less focused than ours, and it is difficult to judge whether the twentieth-century blessings she obtained through voluntary submission are representative of all blessings given during her designated time frame. Nonetheless, we profited a great deal from reading her informative and stimulating study. While there is a certain amount of overlap with Bates's research, our study is based on a systematic statistical comparison of blessings obtained from a more narrowly focused sampling frame that coincides with the emergence of the LDS Church as a new religious movement in America.

H. Michael Marquardt's 2007 publication *Early Patriarchal Blessings of the Church of Jesus Christ of Latter-Day Saints* is a chronological compilation of more than 750 blessings dated from December 18, 1833, through September 11, 1845, which Marquardt has been collecting from various sources for over forty years.[9] Among Marquardt's primary sources is Joseph Smith Sr.'s "Book of Patriarchal Blessings," which contained copies of Father Smith's blessings from 1834 to 1839 and subsequently was used as a record for copying additional blessings bestowed by Hyrum and William between 1843 and 1845. For the years 1840 to 1842, in particular, Marquardt had to rely on a variety of other sources.

Marquardt's compilation is thus not a complete inventory of official patriarchal blessings given to Latter-day Saints during the first decade and a half of their history (hundreds of blessings are unaccounted for), but it includes a substantial proportion of official blessings for that period. It is the single largest collection of early patriarchal blessings available and an invaluable documentary collection for students of new religions in general and Mormon history in particular. Analogous to collections of an artist's repertoire of works displayed in galleries or museums, Marquardt's compilation makes it possible for us to acquire a much deeper understanding and appreciation of the role played by the institution of patriarchal blessings in the doctrinal development of early Mormonism. It represents a fair fraction of the blessings pronounced upon Mormon converts and their children during the stormy Kirtland, Far West, and Nauvoo chapters of LDS history. These early blessings reveal how the Smith patriarchs, through prophetic language, spotlighted and reinforced early Mormonism's most distinctive teachings to Latter-day Saint converts in the face of increasingly fierce and violent opposition to LDS religious heresies and what had developed as a form of economic-political communitarianism on the volatile American frontier.

Marquardt's compilation of early patriarchal blessings makes possible a systematic theme analysis and comparison of recorded blessings issued between 1834 and 1845. The first nine official patriarchal blessings included in Marquardt's compilation actually were bestowed by Joseph Smith Jr. in December 1833 on his father, Joseph Sr.; his mother, Lucy Mack Smith; his four surviving brothers, in order of seniority (Hyrum, Samuel, William, and Don Carlos); and his three counselors in the church's First Presidency (Oliver Cowdery, Frederick G. Williams, and Sidney Rigdon).[10] As prophet, seer, and revelator of the restored church, Joseph Smith occasionally asserted his right to bestow official blessings, including additional blessings recorded in Marquardt's compilation in 1835 and 1843.[11] The prophet's 1833 blessings for his family and counselors were, of course, significant in their own right. Among other things, they established the form and expressive style subsequently employed in the blessings issued to LDS converts by his father and his brothers Hyrum and William.[12]

But since we wish to highlight the part played by other historical actors in the promulgation and development of early Mormonism, we have excluded the relatively small number of patriarchal blessings issued by Joseph Smith Jr. and focus only on those given by his father and brothers in their capacity as presiding church patriarchs. Active as official church patriarch for only four months between his ordination as patriarch in May and excommunication in October 1845, the mercurial William produced a total of 300 blessings recorded in Marquardt's compilation. This compares to Joseph Smith Sr.'s 373 blessings over six years (1834–40) and Hyrum's mere 64 blessings during a four-year period (1840–44). These figures remind us of the incompleteness of Marquardt's collection, especially with regard to Hyrum's blessings at a time when the official patriarchal blessing book had been misplaced. But these comparisons also suggest that William was more prolific at bestowing blessings than his father and older brother. As previously noted, in the early days of LDS history, church members paid the patriarchs a fee for their blessings, so financial remuneration may have been a factor in William's productivity. However, William's blessings were no less articulate or religiously beneficent than those given by his predecessors. If money was a prime motive for William, it is also fair to say that he was serious about his right to bless the people and endeavored to give them their money's worth.[13] In any event, the combined total of 737 blessings attributed to Joseph Sr., Hyrum, and William in Marquardt's compilation constitute our gallery of early LDS patriarchal blessings for the purpose of comparative analysis and interpretation.

SELECTION OF SAMPLE BLESSINGS FOR STATISTICAL ANALYSIS

Traditional historiography depends almost entirely on authenticating and analyzing historically significant documents. Historians' personal and professional competence in deciphering or interpreting thematic meanings—and consequently formulating valid conclusions about historical events from the documentary evidence—is crucial. One way to compare and interpret patriarchal blessings from Marquardt's compilation is to read them all carefully while taking notes on their contents and summarizing what appear to be their modal similarities and differences, excerpting selected texts to validate one's observations. For example, in the previous chapter, our excerpts illustrated the prophetic rhetoric customarily employed by the early LDS patriarchs in their blessings. Our principal approach to the study of these blessings, however, was to perform a statistical content analysis—a standard methodology widely used in social science for systematically analyzing a set of documents. A statistical content analysis requires that we identify a comprehensive list of key words and phrases that appear in the documents under study and then scan every line of every document in order to count the number of times, or frequency, with which these key words and phrases actually occur. Once the relevant frequency counts are made, it is possible to process them so that descriptive and inferential statistics can be calculated to aid researchers' interpretations of the documents.

As with any methodology, content analysis has both strengths and weaknesses. It arguably is a more objective way to evaluate written documents, especially when a relatively large number of documents (such as Marquardt's compilation) constitute a meaningful set of records that can be used to infer group norms and changing social trends. Enhanced objectivity increases the prospects for replicating research findings and, hence, generating greater consensus among researchers. When content analysis methods are used, different researchers can examine the same set of documents and arrive at the same conclusions concerning which group thematic concerns were most or least salient in particular historical periods. The methodology of content analysis, however, is not a mechanical hermeneutic device for revealing definitive meanings. Statistical word counts may help identify central group concerns, but they do not speak for themselves, and they do not replace the necessary insights of trained scholars. They must still be interpreted in cultural and historical context and in conjunction with the knowledge of other relevant documentary sources and the investigators' personal insight shaped through trained experience.

One important methodological decision we made in our study of early patriarchal blessings was to draw a representative *sample* of blessings rather than attempt to survey all 737 blessings in Marquardt's compilation. If a sufficient number of documents is randomly selected for inclusion in a sample, the representativeness of the sample is maximized and can be tested for accuracy by employing "tests of significance." Our criteria for drawing a sample of blessing documents were (1) manageable size—a sample large enough to be representative of Marquardt's entire compilation but small enough for careful and reliable coding; (2) an equal number of blessings given by each patriarch; and (3) an equal number of male and female blessings. We met these criteria by randomly selecting fifteen male and fifteen female blessings given by each patriarch, for a subtotal of thirty blessings per patriarch and an overall total of ninety patriarchal blessings in our sample for the period 1834–45.[14] We then read through all ninety blessings, identifying and recording key words and phrases, which we used to construct an index of the terms used by the Smith patriarchs in their blessings.

Our resultant *theme index* consisted of 431 key words and phrases that constitute the linguistic building blocks for the religious and doctrinal themes expressed in the early patriarchal blessings of the LDS restoration movement.[15] Utilizing the theme index, we systematically scanned every line of every blessing in our sample to numerically code the various themes expressed in the patriarchs' words to different blessing recipients.[16] Once the sample blessings were all coded, we entered them into an SPSS data file for statistical analysis.[17]

In recording word counts, we made the decision to count a word or phrase only once per document. For example, if "inheritance in Zion" was a phrase occurring more than once in a particular blessing, it was only scored once for that blessing. Thus the maximum frequency count for any single word or phrase in our index was ninety, indicating that it appeared in every blessing we examined. Frequency counts give us a way to measure the *relative salience* of particular blessing themes. We infer that blessing themes with high frequency counts in our sample represent some of the most important religious concerns and teachings for early Latter-day Saints, while blessing themes with relatively low frequency counts are indicative of lesser or even idiosyncratic concerns. In the next chapter, we summarize and discuss the most salient themes and corresponding subthemes revealed in our sample of ninety patriarchal blessings issued by Father Smith and his sons Hyrum and William prior to the Latter-day Saints' epic migration to the mountain valleys that encircle the Great Salt Lake.

5

PATRIARCHAL BLESSING THEMES, 1834–1845

To restate our basic thesis: LDS patriarchal blessings emerged as a compensatory commitment mechanism in the prophetic development of early Mormonism. A systematic study of early patriarchal blessings is one way to acquire an appreciation for the distinctive prophetic beliefs of the Mormon restoration that motivated converts to prioritize their religious commitments, forsake their former lives, and, in frequent conflict with detractors and opponents, strengthen their devotion to the realization of what they believed was a transcendent cause. That transcendent cause was building God's Kingdom on earth by preaching the "restored gospel," gathering Latter-day Saint converts to Zion in preparation for the second coming of Jesus Christ, and, after proving themselves worthy of God's commission as his latter-day agents, ultimately attaining salvation and eternal life in the celestial kingdom of heaven for themselves and their posterity.

MAJOR THEMES AND SUBTHEMES
IN EARLY PATRIARCHAL BLESSINGS

To facilitate our study of early patriarchal blessings we have performed a statistical content analysis of a sample of blessings randomly chosen from Michael Marquardt's compilation of *Early Patriarchal Blessings of the Church of Jesus Christ of Latter-Day Saints,* as summarized in the previous chapter. Table 1 shows a rank-order listing of the twenty most frequently

Table 1   Rank order of major blessing themes and subthemes by frequency of mention in a random sample of patriarchal blessings, 1834–1835

Rank	Frequency	Major themes and corresponding subthemes
1	158	*Salvation and eternal life*: celestial crown/glory; celestial kingdom; eternal life/immortality; eternity; salvation; salvation sealed; saved; saved in Kingdom of God; sealed to eternal life
2	148	*Lineage*: (house, seed, descendant of) Abraham; Ephraim; father; husband; Israel; Jacob; Joseph; Manasseh; Zebulon
3	85	*Posterity*: blessed by; a blessing to; blessings of; chosen; inheritance of; numerous; remembered by; special mission of
4	83	*Zion*: city/land of; gathered to; inheritance in; lead others to; Mount Zion; Zion
5	81	*Priesthood*: authority/power of; evangelical; gift of; heir to with husband; higher/Melchizedek; keys of; lineage of; patriarchal; patriarchal right of; priesthood; principles of; rights of
6	80	*Faith*: have been/continue to be faithful; if faithful; increase/ strengthen faith; faithfulness
7	65	*Spirit*: evil; filled with; Holy Ghost/Spirit; Holy Ghost, comfort/guidance of; Holy Spirit of promise; of the Lord/ Truth; power of the; shown by the; spirit(s); spirit prison
8	57	*Affliction*: afflictions; persecution; sorrows; trials; trials given by God
9	52	*Husband*: blessings in common with; calling of; comfort to; lineage of; savior/deliverer; support/obedience to; thy companion; to rule
10	51	*Material blessings*: blessings of health/long life; material/ earthly/temporal blessings
11	50	*Spiritual blessings*: divine reward(s); spiritual blessings
12	49	*Knowledge and understanding*: doctrine/gospel; gift of; mysteries revealed/understanding of; seek/obtain; spiritual; worldly/of men
13	47	*End times*: last days; last days, destruction in; last days, living in; last dispensation; last dispensation, chosen for; Lord, caught up to meet; Lord, coming of; redeemer, live to see; second coming (of Jesus); Son of Man, coming of
14	42	*Israel*: Israel; lineage of; gathering of; house/tribes of; remnants of
15	40	*Good name and reputation*: honored/not forgotten; known among men/nations; name recorded in heaven/in the book
16	38	*Power*: among men; endowed with; over evil/the wicked; over others; spiritual/of God; to convert; to heal; to heal children; to instruct
17	36	*Kingdom*: Lord's; of God on earth; saved in
18	34	*Gospel*: everlasting; fold, brought to; gospel; preach/proclaim; restored
19	33	*Covenants*: covenant people; covenants; everlasting/new; sealed/sealing of
20	30	*Angels*: angels; ministering/guard and protect

NOTE: Subtheme frequencies were summed to produce the total frequencies for major themes.

coded themes (and their corresponding subthemes) in our sample of patriarchal blessings bestowed on Latter-day Saints during the period 1834–45. The corresponding subthemes help specify and clarify the meaning of these major themes and give a clear indication of the primary concerns and doctrinal beliefs shared by both the patriarchs who bestowed the blessings and the church members who received them during this early period of LDS history.

According to our sample results, the most common blessing themes, in rank order of their frequency, were *salvation and eternal life; lineage; posterity; Zion; priesthood; faith; spirit; affliction; husband; material blessings; spiritual blessings; knowledge and understanding; end times; Israel; good name and reputation; power; kingdom; gospel; covenants;* and *angels.* At first glance, most of the major blessing themes identified in our sample appear to be fairly standard religious references within the Judeo-Christian tradition. But in the context of LDS restorationist beliefs, they take on a decidedly Mormon meaning. In Mormonism, the ideology of restorationism functions to justify the distinctive development of LDS institutions and practices in directions that have stimulated charges of substantial heresy from Christian theologians—and the contentious claim by many Protestant evangelicals that Mormonism is, in reality, a non-Christian "cult."[1] From the perspective of restoration ideology, most of the major blessing themes in our sample can, in fact, be recast as distinctive LDS teachings. Thus, for example, our sample's most salient blessing theme—salvation and eternal life—represents a central soteriological concern that is common, in some fashion, to a great many religious traditions worldwide. The Christian tradition in particular has emphasized human salvation through the atoning sacrifice and resurrection of Jesus Christ as its cardinal article of faith. For early Latter-day Saint converts, however, the meaning of Christian salvation and eternal life could not be separated from their acceptance of the prophetic restoration proclaimed by Joseph Smith Jr. In their view, it was only through obedience to the *restored gospel* of Jesus Christ, as authoritatively taught and administered in the *restored church,* that ultimate salvation and eternal life in the presence of God could be assured. The emerging LDS theology of God's plan of salvation, beginning in 1832 with what Richard Bushman has called Joseph Smith's "exaltation revelations,"[2] required the active involvement of his covenant Latter-day Saint disciples both on earth and in a celestialized afterlife.

Directly or indirectly, Mormon soteriology (doctrines of salvation) is at the heart of what is most distinctive and radical in Mormon theology. On the one hand, Mormonism is avowedly Christological and harmonizes with Christian orthodoxy on many points. It emphatically acknowledges the divinity of Jesus Christ, the miraculous atonement of his sacrificial death and resurrection for the salvation of humankind from their sins, and, through followers' pious faith and obedience to Christian precepts, the rewarding promise of eternal life.

At the same time, however, LDS salvation theology specifies an after-life stratified by different kingdoms or "degrees of glory," in which souls saved from sin and death through Christ's atonement can consequently advance toward ultimate deification (or "exaltation") in the celestial king-dom—the highest of the three degrees of glory.[3] This exalted status can only be attained through voluntary compliance with restored priesthood ordinances and covenants, as prophetically revealed by Joseph Smith Jr. Broadcasting this vision and facilitating its latter-day fulfillment is the essential eschatological purpose attributed by Mormons to their reli-gion's nineteenth-century restoration claims. In this recasting of ortho-dox Christology, the atoning sacrifice of Jesus Christ is deemed to be a necessary but not sufficient condition for ultimate spiritual progression and exalted power. Beneficiaries of Christ's grace must subsequently, through their free-will acceptance of and obedience to the restored gospel, *achieve* exaltation through personal merit. As summarized by one Mor-mon theologian, "The meaning of the grace of God through the atone-ment of Christ is that Man by his freedom can now merit salvation."[4] It is this radical theological embellishment of Christian soteriology, so characteristic of the Mormon restoration, that has stimulated charges of flagrant heresy from the nineteenth century to the present day.

For those early Mormon converts who remained most loyal to Smith's new teachings, the increasingly esoteric implications of the new salvation theology, especially in Nauvoo, were justified through their fundamental belief in the restoration of latter-day prophetic guidance and the restored authority of the priesthood to act and officiate in God's name. Authority to officiate in God's name was, of course, also an explicit prerogative of the church patriarch, whose hereditary status by 1840 (when Hyrum assumed the patriarchal office upon the death of Joseph Sr.) was considered to be subordinate only to that of the prophet himself. Through the medium of his blessings, the patriarch was an important expositor of the prophetic doctrines of the restoration as applied to the lives and personal religious concerns of individual church members. As was true for most Christians, chief among Latter-day Saints' concerns was the ultimate fate of their immortal souls. For early LDS converts, eternal life was not only promised in their patriarchal blessings, but it was *sealed* to them (i.e., eternally guaranteed) through the restored priesthood authority of the patriarch. For beleaguered seekers and believers, such authoritative reassurance was priceless. Following the instigation of patriarchal blessings as a distinctive LDS ritual practice, belief in the patriarch's sealing authority functioned as an important institutional and psychological mechanism for reinforcing blessing recipients' religious commitments and their resolve to remain faithful in spite of the many adversities they consequently had to endure.

In conjunction with salvation and eternal life, our sample of blessings also highlights other restoration themes, such as gospel, priesthood, power, covenants, kingdom, spirit, angels, and assorted events associated with the latter-day end times. A full exposition of each of these items would reveal an interconnected set of core LDS beliefs that, when considered through the lens of restorationist ideology, constitute a distinctive Mormon version of the fundamentals of Christian soteriology, ecclesiology, and eschatology. While perhaps less obvious, other salient themes in our sample of blessings also are intimately connected to LDS restoration ideology. Let us revisit, for example, the relatedness of lineage, posterity, Israel, and Zion themes revealed in our sample and their connections with the emergence of early LDS doctrines.

While conflicts periodically erupted between Joseph Jr. and his tempestuous younger brother, William, the Smith family as a whole seems to have placed a high value on their mutual support and family unity.[5] Joseph Jr., in particular, expressed affection and loyalty to his parents and also to his siblings, and he depended on them to support his prophetic narrative and religious authority claims.[6] This may help explain Joseph Jr.'s exposition of lineage and posterity themes in LDS doctrine, as well as their early emphasis in the patriarchal blessings bestowed by his father and his brothers Hyrum and William. In fact, references to lineage and posterity were highly salient themes in our sample of patriarchal blessings, ranking second and third overall in their frequency of mention. But beyond the Smith family's predilection for emphasizing the importance of family and kinship ties, the themes of lineage and posterity were also explicitly linked to core doctrines of the restoration. As we have emphasized previously, the Mormon restoration was not merely proclaimed as the restoration of the primitive apostolic church of Jesus Christ but as the restoration of "all things," especially the covenants and promises to ancient Israel as God's chosen people.

As summarized in chapter 3, early Latter-day Saints assumed the religious identity of a "new Israel," commissioned by God as his chosen people in the last days of human history to fulfill the divine mandate of restoring and implementing the full gospel of Jesus Christ in the plan of human salvation. To Latter-day Saint converts, the full gospel not only meant New Testament teachings but also various Old Testament Hebrew institutions and covenants ordained by God that they believed were never abrogated by the advent of Christianity as a new religious tradition—including temple worship and the practice of plural marriage. Ultimately, and of even greater importance to Latter-day Saints, the fullness of the restored gospel also meant new revelations of God's will and direction, as was evident in Joseph Smith's elaboration of Mormon salvation theology. The ritual aspects of salvation theology became the focal point of LDS temple worship. Accordingly, among the most important and insistent of Joseph Smith's new revelations following Mormon migrations to Kirtland, Missouri, and finally Nauvoo were instructions for building consecrated "temples of the Lord"—not meeting halls for ordinary Sabbath services, but holy edifices in which covenantal endowment ceremonies, and (in Nauvoo) the rites of baptism for the dead, and celestial marriage for time and eternity, could be performed through restored priesthood authority.[7]

As noted previously, patriarchal blessings prophetically informed Latter-day Saint converts of their lineage as direct descendants of the Hebrew patriarchs, especially Abraham and Joseph. They believed that this affirmed them as latter-day remnants of the ancient house of Israel, called out, according to LDS teachings, from the four corners of the earth by Mormon missionaries to gather to Zion—a New Jerusalem on the American continent—where Christ would return to dwell in millennial peace and harmony with his latter-day covenant people.[8] Mormon converts' posterity would be born under God's latter-day covenant; their children's inheritance in Zion would be secured, and the names of their parents would be remembered and blessed by their posterity to the last generation. As exalted beings, their children and children's children ultimately would all be united with them in a celestialized afterlife, in which they would become heirs of God and joint heirs with Jesus Christ. These cardinal doctrinal themes emphasized in early patriarchal blessings illustrate the kinds of ultra-supernatural beliefs which, when rhetorically pronounced upon recipients' heads by patriarchal authority, powerfully reinforced shared commitment and unity of purpose among the faithful.

It is in this context that we can better understand the emphasis given to blessing recipients' "good name and reputation." Not only would blessing recipients be remembered and honored by their posterity in the patriarchal manner of the ancient Hebrews, but they also believed that, as remnants of the House of Israel and chosen bearers of the restored gospel in the last days, they would attain recognition and honor among men and the nations of the world. Ultimately they believed that they were destined to rule with the resurrected Christ and exercise righteous power and dominion in the Kingdom of God on earth.[9] LDS women, too, would actively participate in the building of God's latter-day kingdom, but they would do so in obedience to the male prerogatives of the restored priesthood. Thus, consistent with the patriarchal order of the ancient Hebrews—not to mention the male-dominated structure of nineteenth-century American society—LDS women were told that they would share their husbands' blessings and attain ultimate salvation through the exercise of their husbands' priesthood. (In the next chapter we analyze and comment further on these apparent gender discrepancies in patriarchal blessings.)

Knowledge and understanding were frequently related themes in both men's and women's patriarchal blessings. Most important, to Latter-day Saints, this meant knowledge and understanding of the organizational order of the restored church under the authority of the priesthood of God and the spiritual truths necessary for salvation contained in the restored gospel. Spiritual understanding in particular was couched in ultra-supernatural language and was believed to come through the "gift of the Holy Ghost," bestowed by power of the restored priesthood on each Mormon convert.

It should be noted that in LDS theology the Holy Ghost is considered to be a member of what Mormons prefer to call the Godhead (in lieu of the Trinity). The other two members of the Godhead include God the Eternal Father and the resurrected Jesus Christ, both of whom (unlike the Holy Ghost) possess "glorified," immortal bodies of flesh and blood—which resurrected humans beings also acquire through Christ's atonement. This is not the metaphysical Triune God of Christian orthodoxy. Rooted in Joseph Smith's adolescent theophany, Mormon theology insists that the Father, Son, and Holy Ghost are distinctive, material beings.[10] While unified in thought and action, they constitute a kind of super-ordinate headship organization in which they jointly perform mutually supportive tasks in actualizing the great plan of human salvation. As a spirit rather than corporeal being, the Holy Ghost's designated role in the plan of salvation is to provide comfort to people in times of struggle and loss during their mortal probation on earth; strength in resisting satanic temptation to deny or violate God's laws; spiritual assurance concerning truthful knowledge—especially conviction of the truth of the restored gospel, through which exaltation is attainable; inspiration to make morally correct choices in life; and direct revelation and instruction from God or other departed spirits in resolving portentous religious questions. Thus, through the agency of the Holy Ghost (alternatively referred to in blessings as the Holy Spirit, or God's Spirit), ordinary Latter-day Saint men and women believed that they were entitled to receive inspiration and revelation through dreams, visions, and direct contact with spirit entities. Fully consistent with an ultra-supernatural worldview (in which specified spirit entities are anthropomorphized as supernaturally empowered antagonists who shape the course of human history), they also were told in their blessings that they would be attended by "ministering angels," who would protect them from worldly harm and the destructive wiles of Satan and his evil minions.

At the same time, both men and women were bluntly informed in their blessings that, as converts to the restored church, they would have to suffer sacrificial sorrows and trials to build God's Kingdom; they would be reviled and persecuted for their faith in the restored gospel. They were repeatedly promised, however, that *if they remained faithful,* their sacrifices would be richly rewarded in the end with both the material blessings of an abundant life on earth and all the spiritual blessings of eternal life. These contingent, compensatory promises were essential sources of motivation for early LDS converts, many of whom, in point of fact, were destined to undergo terrible hardship and suffering for their faith. In addition to lost properties, homes, and material possessions, many lost their lives or the lives of their loved ones due to harsh living conditions on the Missouri and Illinois frontiers, violent expulsion from their homes in Far West and Nauvoo, and the arduous journey by wagon, foot, and handcart across the American Great Plains to religious sanctuary in the Rocky Mountains of the Utah Territory.[11] Eternal life was the authoritative promise offered in patriarchal blessings to those who endured to the end, while those who faltered and lost their faith would forfeit their covenantal inheritance.

THEME VARIATIONS IN THE PATRIARCHS' BLESSINGS

While essentially unified in their exposition of core restoration themes in the blessings they bestowed during their respective tenures in office, the

Smith patriarchs also displayed a certain amount of personal (sometimes idiosyncratic) variation in the form and content of their blessings. This is to be expected if we allow for a predictable range of individual differences among human actors in the performance of their roles, especially if their duties permit a certain amount of personal choice and extemporaneous judgment. We have described the issuance of patriarchal blessings as a particular type of religious ritual that, while following a basic procedural format, does not impose rigidly scripted words or specific ideational content, allowing for (indeed, *encouraging*) inspirational, extemporaneous expressions from the patriarch that serve to personalize his blessing to each recipient. At the same time, somewhat distinctive thematic emphases for each patriarch emerge when a sufficient number of their blessings have been analyzed. Some interesting variations appear when we compare the blessing themes most emphasized by each patriarch, as shown in tables 2 and 3.

In table 2, it is the overall range and frequency of William's blessing themes that stand out in comparison to Joseph Sr. and Hyrum. On average, William's blessings were longer in length (see chapter 6) and contained a greater number of salient doctrinal themes when compared to

Table 2 Rank order of major patriarchal blessing themes by patriarch, 1834–1835

		Theme frequencies			
Rank	Major themes	Joseph Sr.	Hyrum	William	Totals
1	Salvation and eternal life	36	45	77	158
2	Lineage	27	47	74	148
3	Posterity	28	33	24	85
4	Zion	20	18	45	83
5	Priesthood	14	41	26	81
6	Faith	23	22	35	80
7	Spirit	17	24	24	65
8	Afflictions	16	14	27	57
9	Husband	15	13	24	52
10	Material blessings	9	31	11	51
11	Spiritual blessings	5	22	23	50
12	Knowledge and understanding	11	19	19	49
13	End times	22	6	19	47
14	Israel	7	11	24	42
15	Good name and reputation	7	17	16	40
16	Power	15	9	14	38
17	Kingdom	8	7	21	36
18	Gospel	9	6	19	34
19	Covenants	5	20	8	33
20	Angels	17	2	11	30

Table 3 Rank order of salient patriarchal blessing subthemes by patriarch, 1834–1835

	Joseph Sr.		Hyrum		William	
Rank	Subthemes	Frequency	Subthemes	Frequency	Subthemes	Frequency
1	Sealed to eternal life	16	Material blessings	22	Lineage of Joseph	28
2	Ministering angels	15	Blessings of health	18	Gathering to Zion	18
3	If faithful	13	Spiritual blessings	17	Have been faithful	15
4	Afflictions	12	If faithful	15	Afflictions	14
5	Blessings of posterity	12	Blessings of posterity	14	Celestial crown/glory	13
6	Blessings in common with husband	9	Lineage of Abraham	13	Father's lineage	13
7	Inheritance in Zion	9	Afflictions	12	Spiritual blessings	13
8	Preach the gospel	8	Sealed to eternal life	12	Salvation sealed	13
9	Material blessings	7	Gift of the Priesthood	11	Lord's Kingdom	13
10	Living in last days	6	Inheritance in Zion	10	Priesthood authority	12

Hyrum or Joseph Sr.'s blessings. Thus, twelve of the twenty most common themes identified in our sample of blessings (salvation and eternal life, lineage, Zion, faith, spirit, affliction, husband, spiritual blessings, knowledge and understanding, Israel, kingdom, and gospel) were more frequently reiterated in William's blessings. In comparison, Hyrum ranked second in the relative frequency of major blessing themes pronounced (posterity, priesthood, spirit, material blessings, knowledge and understanding, good name and reputation, and covenants), while Joseph Sr. was last in his overall mention of the twenty major doctrinal themes in our sample (more frequently referring to end times, power, and angels than either William or Hyrum).

Why William's blessings were both longer and more thematically fulsome on average compared to those of his father and brother is not instantly apparent and even may be somewhat surprising in light of his considerably lesser standing in the historical judgment of both Latter-day Saint and Community of Christ scholars. One could argue that our comparative blessing data reveal certain personality factors at work—that, for example, the mercurial William may have been more effusive in his speech and communication with people in general, while Hyrum and especially Joseph Sr. were characteristically more succinct and focused in theirs. At the same time, an argument can also be made that a linear increase in the relative frequency of major LDS doctrinal themes included in converts' patriarchal blessings demonstrates more than personality differences between the patriarchs: it indicates a developmental group process in which, over time, the central doctrines of a new religion are both elaborated and more firmly emphasized by the group's authorities. This, we suspect, is what our sample of patriarchal blessings most clearly demonstrates. In any event, variation in personal emphasis given to particular religious themes in the patriarchs' blessings does not invalidate or diminish the central finding of our statistical analysis—that their blessings served as a ritual vehicle for reinforcing converts' faith and commitment through a personalized exposition of Mormonism's core beliefs and teachings.

As we anticipated, though our data show some personal differences in thematic emphasis, they also show significant similarities and congruencies in the patriarchs' blessings. This is an important point for understanding doctrinal development and its effective exposition in new religions. In the process of doctrinal development, changes in emphasis also typically occur over time. This is an equally important point for understanding the successful emergence and subsequent organizational advancement of new religions in general. With respect to patriarchal blessing themes, we see, when comparing the first three patriarchs, progressively greater emphasis given to the peculiar Mormon doctrines concerning salvation/eternal life, lineage, and Israel (especially the restoration and literal gathering of Israel in the last days). These themes, in fact, were among the most distinctive doctrinal claims that increasingly separated the Latter-day Saints from other nineteenth-century restorationists.

Personal variations in emphasis as well as the underlying doctrinal unity of the patriarchs' blessings are further specified and illustrated in table 3, which identifies the ten most frequently mentioned subthemes in each patriarch's blessings. In Joseph Sr.'s case we see four signature subthemes (ministering angels, blessings in common with husband, preach the gospel, and living in the last days) that were not among either Hyrum's or William's most frequent blessing references. For William we also find four favored subthemes (have been faithful, celestial crown/glory, father's lineage, and Lord's Kingdom) that do not occur as frequently in the blessings of the other patriarchs. Finally, in Hyrum's blessings we see only one distinctive subtheme (blessings of health).

However, if we shift our attention from the relative salience of different subthemes in each patriarch's blessings to the consensual subthemes that they all emphasized, we find these: gathered to/inheritance in Zion, afflictions, and sealed to salvation/eternal life. Perhaps no other combination of terms from our theme index could be found to better summarize the shared aspirations and expectations of early Mormon converts than these three. The Latter-day Saints' worldly destiny was to gather to and receive their righteous inheritance in Zion, but first there would be afflictions to endure—a sacrificial cost. If they endured their afflictions well, their ultimate compensation would be salvation and eternal life through the sealing power of the restored priesthood.

Once again we are reminded that, at a general level of comparison, there is much in common with the religious worldview of the Latter-day Saints and other Judeo-Christian traditions. There is widespread belief in these traditions that God will materially bless his devout followers who, nonetheless, must be willing to face challenges and make sacrifices for their faith, for which in the end their devotion will be rewarded with some form of salvation or eternal life. But of course, as a new religious movement founded on the basis of Joseph Smith's oracular revelations, these generic religious themes were endowed with the distinctive doctrines of the Mormon restoration. In the next chapter we reexamine prominent restoration themes expressed in early LDS patriarchal blessings in conjunction with yet another highly important group variable: the gender of blessing recipients.

GENDER DIFFERENCES IN EARLY
PATRIARCHAL BLESSINGS

Functional theorists since Emile Durkheim have emphasized the integrative and consensual functions of ritual,[1] while conflict theorists argue that rituals primarily serve a political purpose by reinforcing hierarchical structures of domination. Yet other scholars see rituals as vehicles for contesting and mobilizing resistance to established power.[2] Interpretive disagreements concerning the primary social functions of ritual are not necessarily mutually exclusive. In the Mormon case, for example, it is not difficult to appreciate a mixed reading of the social consequences of patriarchal blessings over time. In Mormonism's early days most converts did not come from wealthy or socially privileged backgrounds. Their regional and national origins were, however, diversified by the far-flung recruitment efforts of Mormon missionaries. By emphasizing egalitarian themes of universal brotherhood in the Zionic community of God's Kingdom on earth, patriarchal blessings served to integrate converts from different cultural backgrounds in a common cause and calling. At the same time, the Mormons' radical doctrinal innovations and theocratic tendencies pitted them against orthodox Christianity and secular authority in nineteenth-century American society. In that context, early patriarchal blessings clearly aimed to contest and mobilize a challenge to established powers.

Within a short time, however, the LDS Church produced its own complex, hierarchical lay priesthood organization that prohibited women and African American males from holding ecclesiastical office. Much later, as racial and gender equality emerged as large-scale social issues in the twentieth century, it may be plausibly inferred that one latent consequence of patriarchal blessings was to furnish both theological justification and practical reinforcement of the exclusive priesthood authority of white Mormon males.[3]

This inference is compatible with I. M. Lewis's cross-cultural analysis of "spirit possession" (which includes belief in visionary revelations and channeling spiritual messages from the beyond).[4] Lewis proposes a distinction between "central," male-dominated possession cults, which reinforce prevailing moral and political institutions, and "peripheral" cults that, through the ecstatic projection of evil and dangerous forces, symbolically protest the oppression of marginalized groups, especially women. While patriarchal blessings are based on the premise of divine revelation, neither in their administration nor reception do they encourage ecstatic performances or experiences in the rapturous, often frenzied modes that Lewis mostly considers. In early Mormonism, particularly during the Kirtland period, ecstatic forms of religious expression were not uncommon (especially the practice of glossolalia), and "blessing meetings" in that period may have been more emotionally expressive than currently is the case, now that blessings are privately bestowed.[5] In any event, while not normally ecstatic, patriarchal blessings in the context of Mormon culture, both past and present, clearly constitute a primary rather than peripheral cultic form. Through the restored priesthood they are exclusively administered by male patriarchs and, while the blessings we analyzed in the last chapter not infrequently contained references to evil oppositional forces, they overwhelmingly reinforced commitment to the doctrines of the restored church.

In the process of propagating and reinforcing member commitment to Mormonism's most distinctive religious claims, were the blessings given to women substantively different from the blessings given men? In particular, did those blessings serve to reinforce women's subservience to male dominance in a patriarchal religious culture? In what follows, we summarize nineteenth-century gender norms in American society and then formulate several hypotheses about gender differences in early LDS patriarchal blessings for statistical testing.

NINETEENTH-CENTURY GENDER NORMS

A surge of feminist studies in history and the social sciences over the past several decades has compelled new interpretations and understandings of our national history and the part that socially constructed gender distinctions play in the process of both maintaining and changing social institutions.[6] Feminist studies of women's roles in nineteenth-century America document the progressive changes in women's social status in the post-revolutionary United States that generated the foundations for the women's movement of the twentieth and twenty-first centuries. From the strict religious and legal subjugation of New England Puritan women to their husbands, to the somewhat more enlightened ideal of "republican motherhood" fostered during and after the American Revolution, and from the assumption of leadership roles in various antebellum moral crusades (such as abolitionism and temperance) to spearheading the long struggle for women's reproductive control and political suffrage, we see women in the nineteenth century increasingly engaged in the process of reconstructing gender role norms in pursuit of social, political, and economic equality with men.[7]

Early nineteenth-century Mormonism cannot be adequately understood apart from the historical context in which it emerged and the larger issues and change trends in nineteenth-century American society, including progressive changes in women's status. Like other topics in American history, Mormon studies have benefited from feminist scholarship in recent decades.[8] The findings of these studies often lead to seemingly ambiguous conclusions about the shaping consequences of Mormonism in the lives of LDS women. On the one hand, some studies of nineteenth-century Mormon women emphasize the relatively liberating consequences of LDS restorationist theology and lay organization for women of that era. On the other hand, Mormonism's early patriarchal emphasis and all-male priesthood structure are frequently viewed as major obstacles to women's equality, especially since the turn of the twentieth century.[9]

What might a systematic analysis of LDS patriarchal blessings reveal about gender norms and the relative status of LDS women in Mormonism's early years as a new religious movement in nineteenth century American society?

HYPOTHESES REGARDING GENDER DIFFERENCES
IN PATRIARCHAL BLESSINGS

By 1830, democratic values reinforced by the American Revolution had already stimulated reconsideration and change in women's status toward greater gender equality, but this was a very gradual historical process and met considerable opposition in both the nineteenth and twentieth centuries. The dominant cultural ethos of the nineteenth century defining women's place in society was the "cult of domesticity" or "true womanhood," in which women were viewed as being naturally more spiritual and obedient than men.[10] Following this line of thought, women would sustain human civilization by maintaining a pious home, raising and cultivating moral values in their children, nurturing and motivating them (as well as their husbands) to pursue virtuous careers in life appropriate to their sex—respectable occupations related to making a living for husbands and sons, and homemaking skills for daughters. The home was idealized as a place of spiritual refuge from the profane world of secular life. Wives and mothers realized their divinely appointed nature by modeling piety for their children and sustaining their husbands, who needed moral support and spiritual reinforcement at home in their pursuit of worldly occupations. In spite of highly significant advances for women over the past century in economic, political, educational, and religious professions outside of the home, these nineteenth-century definitions of gender roles have proven resilient in our own time and continue to be supported by many conservative Christian denominations, including the modern LDS Church.[11]

As a nineteenth-century lay religion that emphasized the restoration of patriarchal priesthood authority, early Mormonism partook of the political and cultural ethos of antebellum American society. To an appreciable extent we should expect to see contemporaneous gender role values and definitions reflected in the early LDS institution of patriarchal blessings. Consciously or unconsciously, were male blessings in any way considered to be more important than blessings given to females? Let us assume this to have been the case and specify some of the implications of a gender-biased cultural ethos for understanding early patriarchal blessings. In a hypothetically extreme case, if inspired blessings from God were considered to be far more important for guiding the lives of men in their priesthood responsibilities than women in their domestic roles, then many more males should have obtained blessings than females. Moreover, female blessings should be much shorter in length than the much more consequential blessings bestowed upon men. And, consistent with traditional marriage norms in which younger women married and were subservient to older men, the age of female blessing recipients would have been significantly younger than for male recipients. Finally, in this case we might also anticipate that when females received their blessings, they would uniformly do so in the company of their husbands, whereas males would be privileged to receive blessings with or without their spouses concurrently receiving theirs.

Based on these suppositions, we formulated the following hypotheses to be tested through an examination of the patriarchal blessings contained in Marquardt's compilation.

H1: Patriarchal blessings were given more frequently to males than to females.

H2: Blessings given to males were, on average, longer in length than blessings given to females.

H3: Male blessing recipients were, on average, older in age than female blessing recipients.

H4: Female blessings were given concurrently with their husbands' blessings, whereas males could receive blessings either concurrently or independently of their wives' blessings.

H5: Blessings given to males were substantively different in content than blessings given to females.

For testing hypotheses 1–4, we examined all 737 blessings included in Marquardt's compilation. Gender frequencies were obtained by simply counting the total number of male and female blessings recorded for Joseph Sr., Hyrum, and William, respectively. Since every blessing record included the recipient's full name, it was not hard to discern female and male blessings. In the few cases of gender-neutral given names (Jesse, Meredith, Peyton, and so on), the patriarchs invariably indicated recipients' gender by addressing them as "sister" or "brother" in their blessings. Blessing lengths were measured by counting the number of lines for each patriarch's blessings; blessing recipients' ages were determined by comparing their birth dates (typically recorded along with their birthplaces) from the dates on which the blessings were recorded. Blessings given to couples in the same place and on the same date were tabulated in a separate category in order to distinguish them from blessings bestowed independently on either male or female recipients.

To test hypothesis 5 concerning *substantive* differences in the content of male and female blessings, we resorted to a systematic content analysis of the sample, as described and discussed previously.

GENDER COMPARISONS FOR BLESSING FREQUENCY, LENGTH, AGE, AND COUPLE STATUS OF BLESSING RECIPIENTS

In tables 4 and 5 we summarize the preliminary results of our statistical comparisons of male and female blessings broken down for each of the Smith patriarchs. Scanning the grand totals for all three patriarchs, we find modest support for hypotheses 1 through 4: table 4 shows that male blessings outnumbered female blessings, 410 to 327 (a difference of 11.2 percent); the mean length of male blessings was 20.1 lines to 17.2 lines for female blessings (an average difference of 2.9 lines per blessing); and the mean age of male blessing recipients was 34.6 years, in comparison to 31.5 years for female recipients (an average difference of 3.1 years of age).[12] Table 5 demonstrates that all three of the patriarchs not only blessed married couples concurrently but also bestowed blessings on both male and female recipients independently, with males receiving independent blessings more frequently than females by a count of 299 to 196 (a difference of 14 percent).

Table 4 Patriarchal blessing recipients' gender, blessing length, and age, by patriarch, 1834–1835

Patriarch	Gender of blessing recipient	Number of blessings	Mean blessing length (in lines)	Mean age of recipient
Joseph Sr.	Male	221 (59.2%)	16.9	35.6
	Female	152 (40.8%)	11.1	30.7
	Total	373	14.6	33.6
Hyrum	Male	34 (53.1%)	21.7	35.8
	Female	30 (46.9%)	16.2	33.4
	Total	64	19.1	34.6
William	Male	155 (51.7%)	24.2	33.2
	Female	145 (48.3%)	23.8	32.0
	Total	300	24.0	32.6
Grand totals	Male	410 (55.6%)	20.1	34.6
	Female	327 (44.4%)	17.2	31.5
	Total	737	18.8	33.2

Table 5 Blessing recipients' couple status and gender, by patriarch, 1834–1835

	Joseph Sr.	Hyrum	William	Grand totals
Married couples	130 (34.9%)	16 (25.0%)	96 (32.0%)	242
Independent males	168 (45.0%)	26 (40.6%)	105 (35.0%)	299
Independent females	75 (20.1%)	22 (34.4%)	99 (33.0%)	196
Totals	373 (100%)	64 (100%)	300 (100%)	737

As anticipated, male blessings were more frequent and typically longer in length than female blessings, and male recipients were older on average than female recipients. However, when we compare male and female blessings for each patriarch, gender differences for all three variables narrow over time—from Joseph Sr. (1834–40), to Hyrum (1840–44), and finally to William (1845). For William's blessings in particular, gender differences with respect to blessings' frequency, their length, and the age of their recipients were very small. Similarly, while males received independent blessings more frequently than females, it was not rare for females to be given blessings independently of male spouses. Furthermore, over time, the relative gender discrepancy in the bestowal of independent blessings progressively declined from 25 percent, under Joseph Sr., to 5 percent under Hyrum, to a mere 2 percent under William. All in all, none of the variables we measured demonstrated an extreme male bias. And what gender differences there were showed signs of diminishing substantially over the first decade of the institution of patriarchal blessings. How surprised should we be by these findings? They provide some modest support for the supposition that male blessings were treated as more important than female blessings, but they might also be read as evidence for emerging egalitarian trends in the early LDS Church.

MAJOR BLESSING THEMES BY RECIPIENTS' GENDER

A statistical assessment of substantive gender differences in the thematic content of patriarchal blessings is a far more challenging task than merely counting blessing frequencies, number of lines per blessing, or calculating the ages of blessing recipients. For this reason we resorted to an analysis of our sample of 90 blessings, consisting of 45 male and 45 female blessings, as described in chapters 3 and 4. Formally stated above, hypothesis 5 predicted substantive differences in the thematic content of male and female blessings. This hypothesis can now be tested by observing how the frequencies of major blessing themes are distributed according to recipients' gender. In table 6 we show the rank order of major blessing themes broken down into separate frequency counts for male and female recipients. Thus, for every theme in the table, we can compare male and female blessings to see how closely their theme counts correspond. Because our male/female comparisons are based on a sample of blessings, we must also conduct tests to determine whether gender differences shown in the sample are statistically significant.[13] A significant difference means that a particular gender comparison in the sample is unlikely to have occurred as a result of random sampling error. Significant thematic gender differences (in which the probability of sample error is either less than 5 percent or 1 percent) are shown in the last column of table 6. We refer to themes that show significant gender differences in our sample as *discrepant* themes, while those that fail to show a significant difference we call *consonant* themes.

Table 6 shows that references to *lineage, Zion, priesthood, Israel, power,* and the *gospel* were significantly more frequent in male blessings than in female blessings and thus were discrepant themes in our sample. These are all important LDS restoration doctrines. While priesthood and power in a patriarchal religion may seem like obviously male-oriented themes, the themes of lineage, Zion, Israel, and the gospel are less so. A closer examination of gospel *subthemes* reveals that the major gender difference here concerned calls to *preach* the gospel, which from the beginning of the LDS restoration was perceived as a male priesthood duty (and remains so

Table 6 Random sample of patriarchal blessings by rank order of major blessing themes and recipients' gender, 1834–1835

Rank	Major themes	Frequencies			Significant difference
		Males	Females	Totals	
1	Salvation and eternal life	77	81	158	—
2	Lineage	88	60	148	P < .01
3	Posterity	46	39	85	—
4	Zion	58	25	83	P < .01
5	Priesthood	47	34	81	P < .05
6	Faith	41	39	80	—
7	Spirit	34	26	60	—
8	Afflictions	27	30	57	—
9	Husband	5	47	52	P < .01
	Material blessings	28	24	52	—
10	Spiritual blessings	23	28	51	—
11	Knowledge and understanding	26	24	50	—
12	End times	29	20	49	—
13	Israel	32	10	42	P < .01
14	Good name and reputation	16	24	40	—
15	Power	29	9	38	P < .01
16	Kingdom	14	20	34	—
	Gospel	27	7	34	P < .01
17	Covenants	15	18	33	—
18	Angels	11	19	30	—

today).[14] On the other hand, references to Zion and Israel overlapped with Mormon millennial beliefs concerning the gathering of God's latter-day covenant people and were ostensibly of equal importance in LDS doctrine for the religious identities of both male and female converts. Why they were given more emphasis in male than female blessings is not at all obvious. Lineage claims of descent through Israel's ancient patriarchs linked Latter-day Saint converts to God's redemptive promises to his chosen people. (While lineage themes were significantly more pronounced in male blessings, we should not lose sight of the fact that they also were among the most frequent themes in female blessings.)

The only discrepant theme in table 6 that occurred significantly more often in female blessings was references to a *husband*, providing at least one very clear example of bias in our sample. This conclusion is further clarified when considering the corresponding subthemes for references to a husband, identified in table 1 (see chapter 5): *blessings in common with; calling of; comfort to; lineage of; savior/deliverer; support/obedience to; thy companion; to rule.* In contrast, references to a *wife*, and corresponding subtheme justifications and admonitions (including "blessings in common with") addressed to male recipients, did not constitute a major theme in our sample of blessings. All in all, there were seven discrepant themes that showed significant gender differences, providing support for hypothesis 5 concerning male bias in patriarchal blessings. At the same time, there were thirteen consonant themes that *failed* to show significant gender differences. Consonant gender themes included *salvation and eternal life, posterity, faith, spirit, afflictions, material blessings, spiritual blessings, knowledge and understanding, end times, good name and reputation, kingdom, covenants,* and *angels.* Thus, in our sample of major patriarchal blessing themes, consonant themes outnumbered discrepant themes by a ratio of almost two to one.

This finding compels us to qualify hasty conclusions about the articulation and reinforcement of male-biased religious values and practices through the powerful institution of prophetic blessings during the Kirtland, Far West, and Nauvoo periods of LDS history. In the most extreme hypothetical case, we can conceptualize a male-dominated religion in which prophetic blessings are bestowed only upon males. In a less extreme case, we can conceptualize a male-dominated religion in which blessings are pronounced upon females, but all or most of the blessing themes exhibit discrepant gender differences. (In contrast, all, or almost all, of the blessing themes in an egalitarian prophetic religion would be consonant with respect to gender.) While early LDS patriarchal blessings were not perfectly egalitarian in their content, they did not exhibit an extreme male-oriented bias, either. More than anything else, consonant blessings for both males and females reinforced Latter-day Saints' shared religious hopes and aspirations regarding the restoration of all things and, as the ultimate reward for their faithful devotion to the requirements of the restored gospel, shared exaltation and eternal life in the celestial Kingdom of God.

SALIENT PATRIARCHAL BLESSING
SUBTHEMES BY RECIPIENTS' GENDER

Our conclusions concerning the relative frequency of major patriarchal blessing themes for male and female recipients are amplified in greater detail by examining the most frequently expressed *subthemes* in our sample of early LDS blessings. Table 7 shows, by rank order, the ten most salient subthemes in male blessings compared to the eleven most salient subthemes expressed in female blessings.

In table 7 we consider *discrepant* subthemes to be those that were salient in the blessings of one gender but not in the blessings of the other. *Consonant* subthemes were those that were salient in the blessings of both male and female recipients. For males, discrepant blessing subthemes included *inheritance in Zion* and *preach the gospel*. For females, discrepant subthemes included *blessings in common with husband, blessings of health/long life*, and *ministering angels*. Thus, hypothesis 5, which predicted substantive gender differences in the content of patriarchal blessings, was supported by a total of five discrepant subthemes.

As we indicated previously, admonitions to "preach the gospel"—a key responsibility of the LDS priesthood—have always been aimed at males. Preaching the gospel was not only associated with recruiting converts and expanding membership but also with organizing and administering new branches, wards, stakes, and other ecclesiastical units of the church, all of which were clearly thought of as male domains. Male ecclesiastical authority and administrative control are, of course, precisely those aspects of institutional religion that most clearly demonstrate structural inequality between men and women in a religious context. However, "inheritance in Zion" was a blessing promised to all faithful Latter-day Saints. What explains its discrepant male salience in patriarchal blessings? We can reasonably speculate that, analogous to reassurances given women that their

Table 7 Rank order of salient patriarchal blessing subthemes, by gender, 1834–1845

	Males			Females	
Rank	Subthemes	Frequency	Rank	Subthemes	Frequency
1	Abraham/Joseph lineage	41	1	Abraham/Joseph lineage	36
2	If faithful	22	2	Blessings in common with husband	25
3	Inheritance in Zion	20	3	Sealed to eternal life	23
4	Material blessings	19	4	Afflictions	20
5	Afflictions	18	5	Blessings of health/long life	19
6	Posterity's blessings	18	6	Material blessings	18
6	Spiritual blessings	17	7	If faithful	16
7	Sealed to eternal life	16		Ministering angels	16
8	Preach gospel	15		Spiritual blessings	16
8	Priesthood authority	15	8	Posterity's blessings	15
				Priesthood authority	15

blessings would be "in common" with their husbands, their inheritance in Zion was also considered to be in common with (or contingent on) their husbands' inheritance. In the first instance, the concept of Zion embodied an actual physical place. It expressed, of course, a spiritual ideal—a place of refuge and deliverance from the corroding sins of the world—but it also meant land and property where the saints of God would dwell in peace and harmony.

According to Richard Bushman, "Zion promised an 'inheritance' to all who migrated there. Fathers who lacked the wealth to provide for their children, as many did in this fast-moving age, were promised land in the holy city. The word 'inheritance' for describing properties in Zion expressed a father's wish to bestow a legacy on his children."[15] In antebellum America, possession and ownership of the land was strictly a male prerogative. For women in general, entitlement to the material benefits of land ownership could only be exercised through their legal relationship to men.[16] Among LDS women in particular, their (and their children's) promised religious inheritance in Zion was linked to marriage with a male priesthood holder.

The most obviously discrepant subtheme for females was, in fact, "blessings in common with your husband." While LDS doctrine emphasizes the unifying importance of marital bonds as a divinely commissioned partnership in God's plan of salvation, no spousal counterpoint contingencies appeared as subthemes in our sample of male patriarchal blessings. Men were not told that their priesthood blessings would be "in common" with their wives, nor, presumably, would their property inheritance in Zion be contingent on having a wife.

The other two discrepant subthemes for female blessings in our sample are less obvious in their gender implications and require additional speculation. Why should blessings of "health and long life" be a more salient blessing subtheme for female recipients? One plausible explanation for this discrepancy lies in the health and morbidity risks faced by women of childbearing age in the centuries before antiseptic medicine and safe, effective birth control measures. Nineteenth-century married couples anticipated having large families, and Mormons in particular placed a high value on numerous progeny who would be born under the covenant of the restored gospel. Women thus potentially faced the prospect of numerous pregnancies over the course of their marital careers, some of which would prove difficult or even fatal. From 1828 to 1842, for example, Joseph's wife

Emma lost three of her babies at birth, and one in infancy; a fourth was stillborn. Emma herself came close to dying after the birth-deaths of her twins in 1828. And both Hyrum and William's first wives (Jerusha and Caroline, respectively) suffered premature deaths while they were still in their childbearing years.[17] We may assume that the early church patriarchs were mindful of the enhanced health-related risks for women during their childbearing years and, perhaps for this reason, they included blessings of health and long life more frequently in female blessings.

Ultra-supernatural belief in angels and their various duties in relationship to mortal human beings was an important aspect of the truth claims made by Latter-day Saints concerning the restoration of the gospel. In LDS ecclesiology, it is the angel Moroni, after all, who appeared to Joseph Smith in order to restore the sacred lost records of ancient America, subsequently published as the Book of Mormon, considered by Mormons to be an essential antecedent to the restoration of the apostolic church. In the restored church, the veil separating mortal life from the spirit world was believed to be unusually permeable, and "ministering angels" were considered to be ever-present sources of supernatural aid and protection for worthy members of both sexes. Why, then, was the reassuring promise of ministering angels bestowed more frequently upon women than men in our sample of patriarchal blessings? In general it may be argued that nineteenth-century LDS women—like their female counterparts in other Christian denominations and society at large—were perceived to be the weaker sex and in greater need of protection. In particular, many faithful LDS males became preoccupied with their missionary assignments and administrative duties, which often took them away from their homes and families for months, if not years, at a time, leaving their wives behind to make ends meet and care for their children. Given the routine absence of husbands and fathers, it is perhaps not surprising that LDS women were promised more frequently than men the comforting blessing of ministering angels. At the same time, pervasive cultural assumptions regarding women's enhanced spiritual sensitivities may also have played a role in male patriarchs bestowing angelic gifts on female blessing recipients.

On the basis of these five discrepant subthemes in early LDS patriarchal blessings, a not surprising male-centered bias is clearly discernable and consistent with the gender norms of nineteenth-century American society. At the same time, we cannot ignore the relatively large number of eight *consonant* subthemes that were salient in the blessings of both men and women in our sample. These included *lineage through Abraham/Joseph, posterity's blessings, afflictions, material blessings, spiritual blessings, sealed to eternal life, priesthood authority,* and (a frequent contingency clause) *if faithful.* As argued earlier, thematic consonance in male and female blessings affords evidence of egalitarian tendencies in the early LDS Church.

The single most salient subtheme in the blessings of both men and women was pronouncement of their lineage through the Old Testament patriarchs, Abraham and/or Joseph.[18] Early LDS stress on the religious importance of lineage and kinship was reinforced for both sexes by frequent references to the future blessings of their *own* posterity. First-generation LDS converts were reassured that, because of their acceptance of and faith in living the restored gospel, their names would be revered by their posterity, and their children's children to the last generation would be blessed as God's covenant people, united in time and eternity as one great family unit.

At the same time, the blessings of both male and female recipients were equally freighted by references to afflictions they had already borne and/or those in life that they would yet be required to endure, presumably as a consequence of their steadfast faith in the restored gospel. Various hardships experienced by converts to new religions in tension with other groups typically are made meaningful by being interpreted as purposeful afflictions, trials, or tests of one's commitment, and they are seen as validations of people's shared faith.[19] In exchange for their sacrificial commitment to the restored gospel, both LDS male and female blessing recipients were promised material as well as spiritual blessings to be obtained in mortality.

Beyond the rewarding promises of a materially prosperous and spiritually uplifting mortal life, the ultimate blessing bestowed upon blessing recipients was, of course, the promise of immortality and eternal life in the celestial Kingdom of God. For Latter-day Saints, to be sealed to eternal life through the restored priesthood authority of the patriarch of the church was, as we previously have emphasized, of inestimable value and represented for both men and women the anchor of their religious faith. All of the promises enumerated in individuals' patriarchal blessings— including the promise of eternal life—were commonly qualified, however, by the phrase "if you remain faithful." One's claims to the promised blessings of God required perseverance in the faith and endurance to the end, no matter what trials, doubts, or afflictions life might bring. Again we can appreciate how bestowal of these blessings served as an important commitment mechanism in early LDS Church history for both male and female converts.

The one consonant subtheme in our sample that initially might seem surprising was "priesthood authority." Not only were males regularly reminded of the authority of their priesthood to act and officiate in God's name, but so, too, were females. One plausible interpretation of this finding is that, while rhetorically consonant for both sexes, blessing references to priesthood served primarily to reinforce the fundamental discrepancy between men's and women's roles in the church: a discrepancy of ecclesiastical power and authority. Consistent with Lewis's characterization of the reinforcing functions of primary cults, the patriarchal blessings' frequent mention of priesthood power and authority highlighted for women their partnership role in the restoration—while emphasizing that they were subject to the ultimate priesthood authority of men.

At the same time, Mormon feminist scholars remind us that the ecclesiastical priesthood divide between men and women in nineteenth-century Mormonism was less substantial and categorical than it became later in the twentieth century. Nineteenth-century Mormon women were "ordained" to positions in the women's Relief Society organization, which, for a time, functioned relatively independently of male priesthood administration. They were granted the gift of healing (especially on behalf of other women and their own children), served as "priestesses" in early LDS temples, and were encouraged to exercise the gifts of prophecy and speaking in/interpreting tongues (none of which is officially condoned today).[20] In many ways, the understandings and gender applications of priesthood power for nineteenth-century Latter-day Saints appear to have been more inclusive than those of today. This may be another reason why priesthood was a more prominent theme in women's blessings of that era.

THE MIXED LEGACY OF PATRIARCHAL
BLESSINGS FOR LDS WOMEN

A summary consideration of all of the findings produced by our content analysis of patriarchal blessings leads to a mixed conclusion regarding gender differences in the early LDS Church from 1834 to 1845. During these early years of church history, more males received blessings than females, their blessings were longer on average, they were older in age than their female counterparts, and they were more likely than women to receive their blessings independently of a spouse. At the same time, the gender differences in these measures turned out to be relatively modest and even showed clear signs of diminishing over time. Similarly, our content analysis of both major blessing themes and their corresponding subthemes showed several important gender discrepancies in the content of members' blessings—with implications for male authority and subordinate roles for women. But gender discrepancies were, in fact, substantially outnumbered by consonant blessing themes that highlighted a shared commitment to Mormonism's highest theological ideals and values as the prophetically restored church of Jesus Christ in the last dispensation of the fullness of time. Thus, while significant gender discrepancies surfaced in our statistical analysis of blessing themes, they did not substantiate hypotheses of extreme male bias.[21]

As we emphasized at the outset of this chapter, to be adequately appreciated, the early record of LDS patriarchal blessings must be considered in historical and cultural context. Male authority themes, whether consciously or unconsciously expressed by early Mormon patriarchs in their blessings to the Latter-day Saints, were quite congruent with both the cultural and legal structures of nineteenth-century American society. But traditional gender norms in the nineteenth century were also in flux and beginning to move in the direction of greater equality for women. Arguably, our sample of patriarchal blessings also mirrored this progressive (albeit gradual) shift. By 1845, LDS women were receiving their patriarchal blessings on par with men in terms of frequency, length, and independence of a spouse. The majority of doctrinal themes expressed in female blessings were consonant, too, with the most salient themes found in male blessings. By and large, these consonant themes centered on Mormonism's most distinctive core beliefs as a new religious movement on the American frontier—beliefs that actively engaged strong women, as well as men, in an exceptionally ambitious religious enterprise.

As Jan Shipps succinctly puts it, "Throughout the nineteenth century, Mormons—women as well as men—were engaged in a restoration venture of monumental proportions."[22] With reference primarily to their post-1845 Nauvoo experience (after a majority of Latter-day Saints had acceded to Brigham Young's authority as successor to the slain prophet of the restoration and followed him to sanctuary in the desert basin of the Rocky Mountains), Shipps goes on to observe,

> As a consequence, perhaps, of their contributions to its restoration, the nineteenth-century Mormon kingdom provided for LDS women

a situation that allowed them a fair measure of independence. They had their own newspaper, the *Woman's Exponent;* they worked for— and during much of the century exercised—suffrage; and, although they never held priesthood offices, they had direct access to the highest levels of ecclesiastical authority through their reasonably autonomous Relief Society. Yet the independence of nineteenth-century sisters should not be misunderstood. The countless diaries and letters of such women extant reveal that the primary concern of LDS women was not independence. Documents such as those included in the recently published collection of Kenneth Godfrey, Audrey M. Godfrey, and Jill Mulvay Derr, *Women's Voices,* show that the lives of most Mormon women were dedicated, as were the lives of the men, first, last, and always to the success of Mormonism.[23]

Congruent with Shipps's broader analysis, we conclude that early patriarchal blessings empowered Latter-day Saints of both sexes with a conviction of their shared duty and imminent destiny in the realization of the egalitarian ideals of Zion and the establishment of God's Kingdom through their belief in the agency of the restored church. Consequently it may be argued that, compared to many other nineteenth-century Christian women, the religious status and active organizational roles of LDS women were relatively progressive for their time and place. Because Mormon society existed primarily on the margins of nineteenth-century American civilization throughout the first forty years or so of its existence, it seems likely that an alternative female role of women making major contributions alongside men to carve out a physically and emotionally challenging life on the frontier was also in play within early Mormonism—especially relative to other religious groups centered in established cities or long-settled communities. Early Mormon women's progress in establishing a more egalitarian gender status, however, became bogged down in the twentieth century, subordinated to a continuation of the previous century's dominant "cult of domesticity." Perhaps this result is partly due to the gradual loss of a Mormon frontier model in which wives functioned as their husbands' strong partners in coping with environmental adversity. In any event, that the increasingly conservative Utah church gradually shifted from what Shipps calls a "radical restoration mode" to a "conservative preservation mode" is a major motif in modern Mormonism's contemporary history.[24]

Do LDS patriarchal blessings today continue to reflect the same mixed patterns of gender discrepancy and consonance revealed by our content analysis of early nineteenth-century blessings? If so, it would reveal the ossification of LDS gender definitions in conformity to nineteenth-century cultural norms. We suspect this to be the case, although obtaining a sampling frame comparable to what Marquardt has compiled for 1834–45, in order to conduct a satisfactory statistical analysis of current patriarchal blessings, would be highly problematic.[25]

LATTER-DAY SAINT PATRIARCHAL BLESSINGS
YESTERDAY AND TODAY

One of the principal assumptions of this book is that new religions that emerge and gain institutional traction in a particular time and place can never be adequately understood as the product of a single religious prodigy or prophetic oracle. Successful new religions are always the product of an interactive social process in which numerous receptive and like-minded individuals converge to construct, mutually, new modes of thought and action. It is a socially creative process. In this process, some individuals, of course, typically contribute substantially more than others to the development of new doctrines and religious norms and to the organizational means for implementing them. But even in prophet-centered religions like the Mormon restoration movement, the prophet is necessarily influenced by and depends on loyal lieutenants to help propagate a new faith. In addition to stalwart lieutenants, successful new religions require the formation of institutional practices that effectively stabilize the authority of the religious community and reinforce members' faith and commitment, particularly when confronted with the concerted disapproval of powerful religious and secular opponents from outside the faith. Such practices may be called group commitment mechanisms, and they are essential to the enduring prospects of any new religion.

At the same time, we should not assume that important commitment mechanisms, once established, are impervious to change. To the contrary: whenever organizations change significantly, we should assume that a particular constellation of previously instituted commitment mechanisms and their relative salience in members' lives are likely to undergo changes as well. Scholars should then endeavor to understand what commitment changes have occurred, why they have occurred, and what their consequences might be for the ongoing life of the community.

Of the many LDS commitment mechanisms instituted over time, we have focused attention on patriarchal blessings as a particularly important ritual practice contributing to the resilience and durability of early Mormonism. As we have argued throughout this book, patriarchal blessings are important in the study of early Mormon development because of their congruence with the LDS restorationist belief in divine guidance through contemporary revelation. Through their kinship ties to the Prophet Joseph and their occupancy, by prophetic fiat, of the institutional office of the patriarch, the Smith patriarchs were considered to be God's anointed agents to bless the people. In their blessings, they presumed to speak for and in the name of God; they claimed the spirit of prophetic revelation to illuminate God's will and project his latter-day purposes in the lives of blessing recipients. They also confidently sealed their blessings and pronouncements both on earth and in heaven through the restored patriarchal priesthood of their office. The supernatural valence attached by believers to the blessings of the patriarchs made the institution of these blessings a unique and powerful commitment mechanism for strengthening the faith of the earliest Latter-day Saints, while simultaneously contributing to the promulgation of the emerging doctrines of the Mormon restoration.

Today, patriarchal blessings are still routinely bestowed upon and cherished by faithful Mormons as a normative step in their lay religious careers. In the Utah-centered LDS Church, patriarchal blessings typically are given to young adults (or adult converts) prior to receiving their temple endowments, contracting a temple marriage, or fulfilling a missionary calling—all of which function as interrelated LDS commitment practices. In this regard, the ordinance of patriarchal blessings has evolved away from functioning as a compensatory commitment mechanism for collectively bolstering the morale of beleaguered LDS converts into a gateway ritual for channeling passage into responsible adult status in the Mormon community. While patriarchal blessings continue to be a distinctive LDS practice, they are now issued to individuals in private settings—usually the patriarch's office at an LDS stake center or personal residence—and they are no longer given by those lineal or lateral descendants of Joseph Smith Sr. who can claim the hereditary office of presiding church patriarch. This

change is partially due to rapid church growth and far greater organizational complexity.[1] What are the social and religious ramifications of these
changes in LDS institutional policy and practice?

FROM PUBLIC TO PRIVATE BLESSINGS

The private patriarchal blessings given to current members of the LDS
Church contrast with the public, communal character of blessings often
bestowed upon early Mormon converts in Ohio, Missouri, and Illinois. As
emphasized in chapter 3, public performances of ritual authority function
particularly to reinforce community bonds and shared commitments. One
plausible historical inference to be drawn from the fact that LDS patriarchal blessings have become privatized is that their commitment function
has changed (if not weakened) over time. One clearly can argue that the
level of commitment required of Latter-day Saint converts in the tumultu-
ous early decades of their history was significantly greater than it is for
most current Mormons. To be a devout Mormon in the nineteenth century
meant to be at odds with the conventional secular and religious institutions of American society and, if necessary, to put at risk one's life, property, and family tranquility in defense of one's religious faith.

Today, however, claiming LDS faith and affiliation is perfectly compatible with active involvement in both the civil and religious arenas of American life and in most other countries around the world. Current Latter-day
Saints are scarcely required to make the kinds of personal sacrifices
endured by their nineteenth-century forebears. LDS accommodations to
the pressures and demands of American legal and cultural institutions
have significantly reduced the sacrificial commitments required of Mormonism's first and second generations. It may be inferred, then, that the
declining community need for resolute commitment in the face of powerful opposition is linked to a decline in the solidarity function of patriarchal
blessings in the lives of Latter-day Saints. In addition, the need for inten-
sive levels of LDS commitment coincidentally declined in historical conjunction with the rise of privacy norms in American culture (as observed
in chapter 4), providing a plausible ex post facto rationale for changes in
the institutional setting of modern patriarchal blessings.

Most significantly, in the context of nineteenth- and twentieth-century
political accommodation, Kathleen Flake shows how and why Mormon theocracy was decisively abandoned following the Reed Smoot hearings from

1903 to 1907. Smoot was a Mormon apostle who, following his election to the U.S. Senate, was denied his seat temporarily by Senate colleagues on the grounds of his organizational connection with, and allegiance to, the sinisterly portrayed LDS hierarchy. Flake argues that "the U.S. Senate's solution to the Mormon problem was a compromise that required the Mormons to conform their kingdom to that most Protestant form of religion, the denomination, with its definitive values of obedience to law, loyalty to the nation, and creedal tolerance. In return, the Senate gave the Latter-day Saints the benefit they sought by sending a representative to the Senate, namely, that form of religious citizenship that provided them protection, at home and abroad, for the propagation of their faith."[2] Flake emphasizes that the tolerance criterion in this agreement—"the privatizing of its truth claims in deference to those of others"—was limited to the political arena.

This was certainly the understanding reached by Mormon officials with the Senate majority who finally voted to sustain Smoot in his senatorial office. But we would add the observation that it also appears to have been an understanding that helped solidify the shift in patriarchal blessings (with their nineteenth-century restorationist emphasis on Latter-day Saints as divinely chosen instruments for realizing the triumphal Kingdom of God on earth) from the public to the private sphere. Mormon accommodation had officially commenced in 1890, when Wilford Woodruff, then LDS president, issued a "manifesto" declaring an end to the performance of church-sanctioned plural marriages. Fifteen years later, as a result of the Smoot hearings, new LDS president Joseph F. Smith issued a "second manifesto" in 1904 reaffirming the cessation of officially sanctioned plural marriages, threatening the excommunication of anyone who advocated otherwise, and forswearing church interference in politics. In 1905, two apostles who had continued performing plural marriages after the 1890 manifesto tendered their resignations and were replaced in the Quorum of the Twelve by monogamists. And in 1910, local stake presidents were instructed to commence disfellowshipping or excommunicating any members who were in violation of the 1904 pronouncement.[3]

With the early twentieth-century church and its leaders in full accommodation mode, one of the corollary changes was a permanent transition from patriarchal blessings issued in public worship services to blessings given to individuals in private settings. For current LDS Church members well integrated in the normative structure of American society, the privatization of their patriarchal blessings now seems perfectly normal and appropriate. The fact that their early predecessors in Mormon history publicly shared theirs in "blessing meetings" would probably come as a surprise to most.[4]

To say that LDS commitment requirements have been reduced historically is not to say that religious identification and relatively demanding commitment levels no longer characterize the Mormon religion. In the denominational context of the twenty-first century, and relative to other religious groups, Mormonism is still in fact a relatively high-demand religion that imposes numerous abstinence and fealty demands and claims on its members' time, energy, and material resources.[5] While significant doctrinal accommodation and social integration within the world's religious economy have been master trends in the modern development of the LDS Church, these trends have been modified and even curtailed by ecclesiastical retrenchment efforts that have channeled Mormonism's course along a conservative rather than progressive path in the twentieth and twenty-first centuries.[6] In this historical process the LDS institution of patriarchal blessings has also undergone substantial changes, including its ritual impact on Mormon solidarity. While still a significant religious event in Latter-day Saints' personal lives, the solidarity function of patriarchal blessings has been eclipsed by the mature development of other LDS ritual practices, especially those performed in LDS temples.

THE CONTEMPORARY RITUAL SALIENCE OF LDS TEMPLES

As stated in previous chapters, LDS temples are not conventional chapels, nor should temple worship be confused with conventional Sunday worship services. LDS temples stand apart from Mormon chapels and, once ritually dedicated, are not open to the public at large.[7] Only baptized members (ordinarily adults) who are deemed worthy by their local bishops and stake presidents may enter the temple to participate in its ritual ceremonies—referred to by Mormons as "temple ordinances." The same sealing power attributed to the Smith patriarchs and emphasized in early patriarchal blessings is the most prominent theological element involved in the performance of LDS temple rituals, which include baptisms for the dead, marriages for time and eternity, and the personal endowment.[8]

Mormons believe that those souls who, in mortality, never had the chance to accept and receive the saving ordinances of the restored gospel may do so in the spirit world through proxy sealing rituals performed in

LDS temples, including marriages and baptisms for deceased ancestors or other persons presumed worthy. For Mormons, ultimate exaltation in a celestialized afterlife requires a temple marriage in which partners are sealed together for eternity as well as the temporal duration of their mortal lives. Prior to being sealed in temple marriage, individuals must first receive their temple "endowment," which is considered to be a spiritual blessing of enlightenment and power that follows a series of vows emphasizing obedience, sacrifice, chastity, and personal consecration to the mission of the restored church. Mormons believe that when conducted in officially dedicated temples, all of these ritual ordinances are validated and sealed through the restored priesthood by authorized "temple workers," making efficacious both on earth and in heaven the covenants and compensatory promises pronounced and symbolically enacted by temple patrons.

While LDS temple ceremonies are closed to outsiders, they are enacted in communion with companies of temple-worthy Latter-day Saints, resulting in mutual reinforcement and unity of commitment to their faith. More than 150 LDS temples around the world are either in use, are currently under construction, or have been officially announced for future construction.[9] All Latter-day Saints are strongly urged to make themselves "temple worthy" so that they can collectively participate in the sealing ceremonies of the restored church. Temple worthiness is operationally defined as compliance with basic member requirements, including confessional belief in the divinity of Jesus Christ and Joseph Smith's standing as God's latter-day prophet of the restoration; belief that the LDS Church is the restored and true church of Jesus Christ; and belief that the current church president is God's prophet on earth. In addition, behavioral compliance is required in pledging submission to the ecclesiastical authority of both general and local officials; marital fidelity; payment of a full 10 percent tithe; abstinence from alcohol, tobacco, and drugs; regular attendance at church meetings; and willingness to accept calls to lay positions in the lay organization of local wards and stakes. Periodic personal interviews conducted by members' local bishops and stake presidents determine whether members are certified or not certified as worthy to enter an LDS temple. For adult Mormons, the maintenance of temple worthiness and regular temple participation now constitute their religion's most salient set of shared commitment mechanisms.

In our analysis of early patriarchal blessings, we have emphasized the way in which those blessings not only united converts in pursuit of the

sacred objectives of their religious faith but also, underscoring the prophetic inspiration of the church patriarch, served to propagate Mormonism's emerging core doctrines. As with the solidarity function of early
patriarchal blessings, though, their doctrinal function has been eclipsed
in modern Mormonism by other institutions, especially the LDS general
conference.

THE CONTEMPORARY SALIENCE OF DOCTRINAL
EXPOSITION IN THE LDS GENERAL CONFERENCE

LDS general conferences today are held biannually in Salt Lake City and
broadcast internationally via television satellite to Mormon wards and
stake centers worldwide. Streamlined and staged for a television audience,
the contemporary institution of general conference has a developmental
history that, like temple worship, also parallels the eventual relative decline
of patriarchal authority in the office of the presiding patriarch.

For the first decade of Mormon history, the movement's leading elders
participated in periodic but irregular conferences, which were convened,
as needed, to deliberate the organizational, doctrinal, and economic concerns of a new religious movement. These early conferences served a number of important organizational functions associated with the governance
of the church and the administration of both its internal and external
affairs: in the conferences, church leaders commonly debated policies,
formulated organizational goals, made decisions, performed religious
ordinances (such as baptisms and ordinations to offices in the Mormon
priesthood), and exercised church discipline through censure, disfellow-
shipment, or excommunication proceedings. The preaching of sermons
was often incidental to the conduct of church business and administrative
tasks at early Mormon conferences.

With the passage of time and the development of other forms of church
organization, LDS conference patterns became increasingly routinized.
The institution of annual and semiannual conferences convened for the
benefit of the entire church membership emerged as an established pattern around 1840 and has been followed ever since.[10] Increasingly, general
conferences provided Mormon leaders with a vehicle for the public exposition of new religious doctrines and the opportunity to exhort rank-and-file
members to strengthen their commitment to the faith. Adherence to a
regular schedule meant that general conference was not merely an ad hoc

way of responding to immediate crises, but that it had become an institutionalized mechanism for charting and steering the course of an enduring
religious movement. General conference eventually became an anticipated
ritual event for both leaders and rank-and-file members, celebrated as a
stable reference point in the life of the Mormon community for reinforcing commitment and preserving institutional coherence.

The routinization of a conference schedule was accompanied by the
specialization of conference functions. Business once conducted at general
conference became the primary task of newly organized church councils
and priesthood quorums, such as the First Presidency, the Quorum of the
Twelve Apostles, the High Council, School of the Prophets, and the Council of Fifty—all instituted between 1832 and 1844. One consequence of
these organizational developments was to divest general conference of
most of its earlier governance and administrative functions while, at the
same time, increasing the importance of its indoctrinational character.
Unencumbered by administrative concerns, conference time could be
devoted almost entirely to the exposition and defense of Mormon doctrine,
to the denunciation of the church's enemies, and to the exhortation and
admonition of church members by the movement's ecclesiastical authorities. Rather than a place where policies might be debated and decisions
made, conference became chiefly a place where the authority of the
church, and hence of its leaders, could be legitimated and strengthened.
Conference administrative proceedings were gradually reduced to pro
forma "votes" for the purpose of sustaining leaders called to important
positions in the hierarchy and to the ritualistic approval of policies formulated prior to conference by the governing councils of the church.[11]

Today, in addition to being televised, general conference talks given
by LDS general authorities are published in church periodicals for mass
distribution to a worldwide membership. Many of these talks are included
annually as reference sources in the church's lesson manuals for various
auxiliary teaching organizations, such as Sunday school classes, male
priesthood quorums, and women's Relief Society courses of study. Rank
and file members consider general conference pronouncements on doctrine and church policy to be authoritative and frequently quote or reference them in lay sermons for delivery in their local congregations. In
contrast, while typically consistent with core LDS beliefs, current patriarchal blessing pronouncements are considered to be personalized directives
to individual members and are seldom quoted in public to either support
or expound church doctrine. Over time, the privatization of patriarchal

blessings has become inversely correlated with the public broadcast and management of the LDS Church's contemporary image as an influential denomination in the world's religious economy.[12]

It should be noted here that religious solidarity, commitment, and doctrinal exposition are not mutually exclusive outcomes confined to separate church organizations or specific ritual practices. In Mormonism, all three of these functions have been served, in varying degrees, by temple participation and general conference proceedings as well as through patriarchal blessings. Our analysis leads to the conclusion, however, that the salience of LDS temples and general conference in these basic areas of Mormon group life has progressively increased over time, while the relative commitment, solidarity, and doctrinal exposition salience of patriarchal blessings has correspondingly declined. One important correlate of this relative decline has been the virtual extinction of the hereditary office of the church patriarch.

THE DECLINE OF THE OFFICE OF PRESIDING CHURCH PATRIARCH

In neither the LDS Church nor the Community of Christ are patriarchal blessings still given by the presiding patriarch to the church, whose singular prophetic standing through lineal descent has been discarded in the face of rapid church growth and far greater organizational complexity in both denominations. A history of the institutional conflict generated by the anomalous hereditary office of the church patriarch within the context of an emerging, bureaucratic ecclesiastical organization has been skillfully narrated and analyzed by Irene M. Bates and E. Gary Smith in their book *Lost Legacy: The Mormon Office of Presiding Patriarch*—a book in which they employ Max Weber's theory of the "routinization of charisma" in maturing new religions whose origins are based on the prophetic claims of charismatic founders.[13]

According to Weber, in order to endure beyond the demise or departure of a charismatic founder, successful new religions must develop authority hierarchies and formal institutional practices to provide organizational stability and generational continuity. The personal charisma of the founder is transformed by a process Weber called the "routinization of charisma," resulting in what may be called "charisma of office." Member respect and devotion become attached to an office, or set of offices, in an organizational hierarchy. Whoever subsequently occupies these offices—whether through legitimate methods of election, appointment, or seniority—is set apart and commands the charismatic authority of the office, regardless of his or her personal leadership qualities. A fourth method for transferring charismatic authority is through hereditary kinship to a group's founder. Hereditary authority is the norm in traditional societies, but is out of sync with credentialed achievement norms in modern meritocracies. The position of presiding church patriarch was not only designated as a hereditary office by Joseph Smith prior to his assassination, but it was also an office invested with charismatic prophetic authority to pronounce God's word in blessing the people. This placed the authority of the patriarch in an ambiguous relationship to the supreme ecclesiastical authority of the Prophet, the First Presidency, and the Quorum of the Twelve Apostles.

The Quorum of the Twelve is a self-selecting, elite collegial group that, since the days of Brigham Young, has provided the LDS Church with an executive leadership organization. Elevation to this group is based on "calls" or appointments made upon the deaths of previous apostles (who are appointed for life) through prayerful discussion and consensus vote by existing quorum members. Individuals chosen as replacement apostles invariably have promising records of religious service and loyalty within the lay ranks of the Mormon priesthood. After lengthy years of ecclesiastical service, it is the senior apostle who is next in line to become the president (and titular Prophet) of the church upon the death of the previous incumbent. A new church president is then entitled to choose his own counselors to serve in the First Presidency, which is the apex of the LDS priesthood hierarchy. In the LDS faith tradition, callings to the apostleship and/or the First Presidency are considered to be the result of divine inspiration, and all those who occupy these offices—especially the church president—are considered to be "prophets, seers, and revelators." Their official statements of church policy, or pronouncements on church doctrine (often delivered at general conferences), are regarded by Latter-day Saints to be the primary expressions of God's will and guidance for the contemporary world.

The institutional history and contemporary administrative modes of functioning of the Quorum of the Twelve Apostles and the First Presidency are examined at length by D. Michael Quinn.[14] While Quinn documents the considerable extent to which LDS general authorities are connected by kinship and marriage, he also shows how long years of

church service and lay activity (typically supplemented by prior training and secular occupations in such fields as business, law, and church
education) supply them with meritorious credentials for administrative
leadership. What emerges in Quinn's analysis is a human portrait of conservative religious leaders in a hierarchical church organization who,
much like the directors of any large corporation, lobby their colleagues,
jockey for influence, forge alliances, and negotiate compromises. This view
of the inner workings of the LDS hierarchy is substantially confirmed by
Greg Prince and Robert Wright's detailed documentary description of the
"rise of modern Mormonism" during the post–World War II administration of Church President David O. McKay.[15] While often divided in their
personal views, and very cautious in encouraging or sanctioning oracular
visionary experiences as routine grounds for making organizational decisions, LDS general authorities predictably pull together in unanimity when
they collectively believe that God has revealed his will to them on momentous matters of church doctrine or policy. In a previous study of the transition from oracular to inspirational prophecy in modern Mormonism, we
quote a knowledgeable informant who concludes that the way in which
most contemporary LDS policies, official programs, or doctrinal pronouncements are promulgated is

> not so different from the usual committee process that occurs in
> various complex organizations, especially voluntary ones, including
> religious denominations. In actual practice a lot of participation
> occurs, not only up and down the LDS hierarchy, but up and down
> the professional bureaucracy that advises the hierarchy. Having been
> a participant myself on several ad hoc committees advising the LDS
> hierarchy and the bureaucracy at various levels, I have seen the proc-
> ess at work: A need for a new policy, program, or even scripture
> might be identified by the First Presidency or the Twelve (or both).
> The next echelons—the Seventy or perhaps Presiding Bishopric or
> General Relief Society [other organizational divisions in the LDS
> hierarchy]—will be asked to take the matter under advisement, and
> they typically will delegate to their paid professional staffs (and/or ad
> hoc committees recruited through the professional staffs) the
> responsibility for conducting the research and preparing the propos-
> als that will be sent up the leadership chain, where some of them
> will eventuate in "inspired utterances" from top priesthood leaders.

These utterances can take the form of letters from the First Presidency or from the Twelve, or (in rare cases) the addition of sections to the Doctrine and Covenants. Even the lesson manuals in the church curriculum carry the presumption of divine inspiration. All such are considered to have been received by "revelation," since they are products of the promptings of the Holy Spirit and carry the imprimatur of the President of the Church, who is the living prophet.[16]

Subsequent to the tenures of Hyrum and William Smith as hereditary patriarchs to the church, successor church patriarchs were never called as members of the Quorum of the Twelve. Their office was detached from the centralized leadership organization of the church; they were not part of a collegial administrative group whose appointments were based on proven performance criteria. Yet as patriarchs, their hereditary prophetic authority potentially rivaled that of the apostles. Bates and Smith have detailed the history of the ambiguous relationship between the hereditary office of presiding church patriarch and the appointment-based seniority system of the Quorum of the Twelve. The history of this relationship demonstrates a steady curtailment of the institutional role and authority of the church patriarch—a history whose ultimate denouement arrived in 1979, when LDS President Spencer Kimball unceremoniously announced at general conference that then Church Patriarch Eldred G. Smith was to be designated as "Patriarch Emeritus." This action constituted an imposed retirement on Patriarch Smith from his official hereditary position.[17] From that time on, no one has occupied or executed the office of presiding church patriarch. For all practical purposes, this once-revered office has been discarded from the ecclesiastical structure of the modern LDS Church.

CONCLUSION

Human institutions, including religious institutions, are subject to a wide assortment of interrelated changes over time in which the stabilizing authority and functions of venerable group practices may be modified, supplemented, or superseded by new institutional forms.[18] This elementary fact of social life is highlighted in the history of the office of church patriarch and the ritual practice of bestowing patriarchal blessings in the

LDS Church. In the presiding patriarch's stead today, hundreds of stake patriarchs administer tens of thousands of blessings annually to church members residing in LDS stakes throughout the world.[19] No longer under the general jurisdiction of a presiding patriarch, stake patriarchs are subject to the local authority of LDS stake presidents and have been given standard guidelines to follow in administering their blessings.[20]

Here, in the institution of LDS patriarchal blessings, we see a clear example of the routinization of charisma in new religions that not only survive the hazards of their origins but, over successive generations, also grow and even flourish by making accommodating adjustments in their doctrines and organizational practices. In the Mormon case, this process has featured a transition from the strong charisma of Joseph Smith's early oracular revelations to increasing reliance on the milder and less polarizing charisma of inspirational guidance, which is closely regulated by an ecclesiastical hierarchy. Diminution and eventual elimination of the office of presiding church patriarch and increasing standardization and regulation of patriarchal blessings has been a significant part of this transition process.

Institutional routinization and current organizational controls notwithstanding, patriarchal blessings issued privately by local stake patriarchs are still considered by devout Latter-day Saints to be inspired by God. As was true for their nineteenth-century forebears, LDS members continue to take them seriously as an enduring source of comfort and religious guidance in their lives. Even though their relative salience as a ritual means for uniting the faithful and promulgating prophetic doctrines has diminished, patriarchal blessings today, as in the past, continue to serve as a meaningful anchor of personal commitment in the religion of the Latter-day Saints.

Based on her comparative reading of an assortment of both nineteenth- and twentieth-century patriarchal blessings, Irene Bates concludes that "in the twentieth century most of the more extravagant promises [contained in nineteenth-century patriarchal blessings] appear to have disappeared in blessings to both men and women. While it is true that [current] patriarchs have been cautioned to be more conservative in their blessings to avoid possible damage to faith, some of the changes can be seen as reflections of cultural change." (This, of course, is precisely one of our own guiding assumptions.) Bates goes on to say that most of the twentieth-century blessings in her sample for both males and females focused on such things as church service, education, gender roles, and directions for family life, "plus the traditional statement of lineage and the promise that recipients will come forth on the morning of the first resurrection, clothed in glory, immortality, and eternal life."[21]

The patriarchal blessings of devout Mormons in the twenty-first century are of a piece with their missionary experiences, temple marriages and family sealings, and their anticipation of what they believe are inspired directives from the apostles and current prophet-president at biannual general conferences of the LDS Church. All of these institutional elements converge to reinforce member religious commitments as Latter-day Saints in the contemporary world.[22] Although modified and peculiarly adapted to the conservative flanks of American cultural and political life in the twenty-first century, adherence to elements of Mormonism's nineteenth-century oracular foundations nonetheless continues to set Mormons apart as members of a distinctive faith tradition in the world's religious economy.

APPENDIX A

Examples of Oracular Versus Inspirational Modes of Prophetic Rhetoric Recorded in the LDS Doctrine and Covenants

Selected Joseph Smith Pronouncements

MARCH 1830: "I am Alpha and Omega, Christ the Lord; yea, even I am he, the beginning and the end, the Redeemer of the world. . . . I command you to repent, and keep the commandments which you have received by the hand of my servant Joseph Smith, Jun., in my name." (D&C 19:1, 13)

APRIL 6, 1830: "Behold, there shall be a record kept among you; and in it thou [Joseph Smith] shalt be called a seer, a translator, a prophet, an apostle of Jesus Christ, an elder of the church through the will of God the Father, and the grace of your Lord Jesus Christ, being inspired of the Holy Ghost to lay the foundation thereof. . . . Wherefore thou shalt give heed unto all his words and commandments which he [Joseph Smith] shall give unto you as he receiveth them. . . . For his word ye shall receive, as if from mine own mouth." (D&C 21:1–5)

NOVEMBER 1, 1831: "Hearken, O ye people of my church, saith the voice of him who dwells on high . . . the voice of warning shall be unto all people, by the mouths of my disciples, whom I have chosen in these last days. And they shall go forth and none shall stay them, for I the Lord have commanded them. Behold, this is mine authority, and the authority of my servants, and my preface unto the book of my commandments, which I have given them to publish unto you, O inhabitants of the earth." (D&C 1:1–6)

JANUARY 19, 1841: "Let this house [the Nauvoo Temple] be built unto my name that I may reveal mine ordinances therein unto my people; for I deign to reveal unto my church things which have been kept hid from before the foundation of the world, things that pertain to the dispensation of the fullness of times. And I will show unto my servant Joseph all things pertaining to this house, and the priesthood thereof." (D&C 124:40–42)

JULY 12, 1843: "Verily, thus saith the Lord unto you my servant Joseph, that inasmuch as you have inquired of my hand to know and understand wherein I, the Lord, justified my servants Abraham, Isaac, and Jacob, as also Moses, David and Solomon, my servants, as touching the principle and doctrine of their having many wives and concubines . . . prepare thy heart to receive and obey the instructions which I am about to give unto you. . . . I reveal unto you a new and an everlasting covenant; and if ye abide not that covenant, then are ye damned; for no one can reject this covenant and be permitted to enter into my glory." (D&C 132:1–4)

Selected Post–Joseph Smith Pronouncements

JANUARY 14, 1847: "The Word and Will of the Lord concerning the Camp of Israel in their journeyings to the West: Let all the people of the Church of Jesus Christ of Latter-day Saints, and those who journey with them, be organized into companies, with a covenant and promise to keep all the commandments and statutes of the Lord our God. Let the companies be organized with captains of hundreds, captains of fifties, and captains of tens, with a president and two counselors at their head, under the direction of the Twelve apostles. And this shall be our covenant—that we will walk in all the ordinances of the Lord." (D&C 136:1–4)

OCTOBER 6, 1890: "I [Wilford Woodruff], therefore, as President of the Church of Jesus Christ of Latter-day Saints, do hereby, in the most solemn manner, declare. . . . Inasmuch as laws have been enacted by Congress forbidding plural marriages, which laws have been pronounced constitutional by the court of last resort, I hereby declare my intention to submit to those laws, and to use my influence with the members of the Church over which I preside to have them do likewise. . . . And I now publicly declare that my advice to the Latter-day Saints is to refrain from contracting any marriage forbidden by the law of the land." (D&C Official Declaration 1)

JUNE 8, 1978: "Aware of the promises made by the prophets and presidents of the Church who have preceded us that at some time, in God's eternal plan, all of our brethren who are worthy may receive the priesthood . . . we [The First Presidency] have pleaded long and earnestly . . . spending many hours in the Upper Room of the Temple supplicating the Lord for divine guidance. He has heard our prayers, and by revelation has con-firmed that the long-promised day has come when every faithful, worthy man in the Church may receive the holy priesthood. . . . Accordingly, all worthy male members of the Church may be ordained to the priesthood without regard for race or color." (D&C Official Declaration 2)

Blessings Randomly Sampled from Michael Marquardt's *Early Patriarchal Blessings of the Church of Jesus Christ of Latter-day Saints*

Joseph Smith Sr.'s Blessings, by Recipient and Date

Jerusha Smith, December 9, 1834
Hyrum Smith, December 9, 1834
Almon Sherman, April 3, 1835
Susan Sherman, April 3, 1835
Amos F. Herrick, July 1, 1835
Sidney Rigdon, September 14, 1835
Elizabeth A. Whitney, September 14, 1835
Lyman Wight, December 29, 1835
Caroline Crosby, February 21, 1836
William Harris, May 2, 1836
Abigail McBride, June 8, 1836
Jeremy Bartlett, June 25, 1836
Mary A. Baldwin, November 2, 1836
Lorenzo Snow, December 15, 1836
Sarah Thompson (not dated, but 1835 or 1836)
Juliza Chapman (not dated, but probably 1836)
Moses Clawson (not dated, but probably 1836)
Betsey Davison (not dated, but probably 1836)
Simon Dyke (not dated, but probably 1836)
Charlotte Isham (not dated, but probably 1836)
John Lawson (not dated, but probably 1836)
Mary Nelson (not dated, but probably 1836)
Jonas Putnam (not dated, but probably 1836)
Rebecca Smith (not dated, but probably 1836)
Elisha T. Ward (not dated, but probably 1836)
Desdamona Fulmer, February 9, 1837
Levi Richards, April 15, 1837
John Dickson, October 23, 1837
Sophia Packard, December 13, 1837
Margaret Johnston, February 5, 1839

Hyrum Smith's Blessings, by Recipient and Date

John C. Bennett, September 14, 1840
Phebe Merrill, January 2, 1841
Samuel Merrill, January 2, 1841
William I. Appleby, May 7, 1841
Mary Newberry, May 30, 1841
Susanna White, September 8, 1841
Levi Graybill, October 4, 1841
Polly Graybill, October 4, 1841
Hannah M. E. Harris, November 12, 1841
William Ford, November 17, 1841
Edward Phillips, December 20, 1841
James Pace, January 10, 1842
Lucinda Pace, January 10, 1842
Urban Van Stewart, February 9, 1842
Jane A. Twist, February 11, 1842
Heber C. Kimball, March 9, 1842
Elizabeth D. Bushman, March 12, 1843
Addison Pratt, March 28, 1843
Anne Harmon, June 6, 1843
Jesse P. Harmon, June 6, 1843
Frances Crosby, July 18, 1843
Sylvia A. Carter, September 17, 1843
Howard Egan, September 24, 1843
Ann E. DeLong, October 16, 1843
Miles Anderson, November 12, 1843
Sarah M. Pratt, December 26, 1843
Elisha H. Groves, January 8, 1844
Sarah F. Zundel, January 21, 1844
William R. R. Stowell, January 31, 1844
Mary I. Horne, April 2, 1844

William Smith's Blessings, by Recipient and Date

James Lawson, June 6, 1845
Elizabeth Packer, June 19, 1845
James Potter, June 24, 1845

Constantia Hutchison, June 25, 1845
Mary Lambert (probably June 1845)
William McKown (probably June 1845)
Jonathan Packer (probably June 1845)
Hannah M. McNitt, July 3, 1845
Thomas Crompton, July 7, 1845
Mary Gardner, July 7, 1845
Margaret Boyd, July 9, 1845
Lorenzo A. Quick, July 11, 1845
David Wilkie, July 14, 1845
Isabella Wilkie, July 14, 1845
George Black, July 17, 1845
Alexander Walker, July 23, 1845
Susan Younger, July 23, 1845
Henry Moore, July 28, 1845
Elizabeth Merrill, July 29, 1845
Lorenzo Pettit, July 30, 1845
Albina M. Williams, July 30, 1845
Shorson Simpson, August 4, 1845
Mary Simpson, August 4, 1845
Alison McNeil, August 6, 1845
Alexander Allen, August 11, 1845
Matilda Bassett, August 15, 1845
Samuel E. Hull, August 18, 1845
Mary J. Warner, August 25, 1845
Richard Bender, September 1, 1845
Lucinda West, September 9, 1845

APPENDIX C

Thematic Word Index for Patriarchal Blessings

Aaron, rod of
Abraham
Abraham, lineage of
abundance (material possessions)
account/accountable
Adam
Adam, choice of
Adam, sin of
Adamondi-ahman
affliction
Almighty, the
Ancient of Days
angel(s)
angel, destroying
angel (of the Lord)
angels, ministering of
anger
anger, just/righteous
anointed
approbation
avenge
authority
benevolence
blessed (by posterity)
blessed (in his generations)
blessed (of the Lord)
blessing, Father's
blessing(s), seal/sealed
blessing (to posterity)
blessings, earthly/material
blessings (of fathers')
blessings (of Heaven)

blessings (of Joseph)
blessings (of labor)
bondage
bondage, delivered from
broken in heart/spirit
burden(s)
called/calling
calling, magnify
celestial kingdom
children
children (a comfort to)
children, blessed with
children, bring forth
children, guidance of
children's children
choice (chosen)
chosen vessel
Church, the
Church of the Latter-day Saints
comfort/comforted
command the elements
commandments
commandments, keep/keeping
commandments, obey
commandments, teach
consolation
council(s)
council (of the elders)
counsel
covenant(s)
covenant, new and everlasting
covenant (people)

covenant, sealed/sealing of

dead, raise the

dead, resurrection of

death, not taste of

deliver/deliverance

descendant

devil(s)

devil, ensnarement of

diligence

dispensation(s)

dispensation, last (chosen for)

dispensation, last/fullness of times

dream(s)

earth, the

earth, renewal of

education, seek/obtain

elect (the)

endowed/endowment (from on
   high)

enemies/adversaries

enemies, avenge

enemies, delivered/protection from

enemies, dominion of

enemies, escape from

enemies (power/triumph over)

enemies, put to flight

enemies (repay/vengeance against)

enemies (under his/their feet)

Enoch

ensign

Ephraim

Ephraim, lineage/house of

Ephraim, sons of

Ephraimite ("thou art")

error(s)

escape

esteem

eternal glory

eternal life

eternal life (inherit crown of)

eternal life, sealed to

eternal life, shall have

eternity

evangelist

faithful, continue

faithfulness

family

fast/fasting

father(s)

father, duties of

Father's family

Father's family, place in

fearlessness

fellowship

flesh, the

fold, brought to

folly/follies

foolish/foolishness

forgive/forgiveness

friend/friendship

Garden of Eden

Gentile(s)

Gentile nations

Gentiles, fullness of

God, condescension of

God, dwell in presence of

God, judgment of

God, power of

God of Abraham, Israel, Jacob, etc.

God of Israel

God's anger

God's voice

God's word

good things of the earth

gospel

gospel, everlasting

gospel, for the sake of

gospel, preach

law(s)

law(s) of God

law(s) of land/man

lawgiver(s)

lawyer(s)

lawyer (in Israel)

legislature(s)/legislative bodies

liberality (of soul/generousness)

Lord, blessed of

Lord, Book of the

Lord, caught up to meet

Lord, coming of (Christ, Redeemer)

Lord, law of

Lord, loved of

Lord, of glory

Lord (of Sabaoth)

Lord, watch over

Lord, will of

Lord, word of

Lord, work of

Lord Jesus Christ

Lord/Redeemer, shall see

Lord's Kingdom, bring souls to

Lost Tribes, gathering of

magnified (among men)

magnify (calling)

magnify (God/Lord)

magnify (priesthood)

marvelous work and wonder

meek/meekness

mercy

Messiah

Michael (Archangel)

millennial reign (of Jesus)

mind

mind, troubled

ministry

miracles, perform

miracles, witness

mission

mission of the Lord

mortality

mother(s)

Mother in Heaven

Mother in Israel

mother of many children

mothers, duties/responsibilities of

mysteries, understanding of

name, recorded/written in Heaven/
    Book

nations/foreign nations

Nephites

nobility

nobles of the earth

obedient/obedience

obedient son

offspring

old age, live to

oppressed

oppressor(s)

ordain/ordained

Patriarch(s)

patriarchal blessing(s)

patriarchs (assembly/council of)

peace

persecute/persecution

persecutor(s)

philanthropy

polished shaft

poor, the/needy

posterity

posterity, blessing to

posterity, numerous

posterity, special mission of

power (from on high)

power (over others)

power (to instruct)

prayer(s)

prayer(s), Lord will hear

predict

pre-existence

presidency of the church

prevail

pride

priestess

priestess (to rule with husband)

priesthood

priesthood, conferral of

priesthood, evangelical

priesthood, everlasting

priesthood, heir to with husband

priesthood, higher (Melchizedek)

priesthood, holy

priesthood, honor

priesthood, lesser (Aaronic)

priesthood, magnify

priesthood, Patriarchal

priesthood, Patriarchal, right of

priesthood, principles of

priesthood, right(s) of

priesthood, sealed upon

prince (over them)

progenitor(s)

Promised Land

prophecy

prophecy, spirit of

prophesy

prophet(s)

prophet, school of

prophets, avenge blood of

prosperity

providence

purpose, Divine

queen (will be a)

rebel/rebelled

rebuke

record(ed), in the Book

records

Redeemer

Redeemer, live to see

redemption

rejoice/rejoicing

remnants

repent/repentance

repent, need to

reproach

respect

resurrection, come forth on first
    morn

reward(s)

riches (gold, silver, etc.)

righteous

righteousness

rulers (will be)

saints, the

saints, inheritance among/with

salvation

salvation sealed

Satan

Satan (power of)

saved

saved (in the Kingdom of God)

second coming, remain until

seed

seed, chosen

seer

seer, choice/chosen

shame

sick, blessing/healing of

sickness

sign(s) of the times

signs to the nations

sorrow(s)

soul

spirit(s)

spirit(s), choice

spirit, evil
Spirit (of the Lord)
spirit world
spokesman (to the Lord)
spread/spreading abroad
steadfastness
strength
suffer/suffered
talent(s)
teach children
teach those of thy sex (women)
teacher
tears
tears (of joy)
tears (of sorrow)
testimony
throng, heavenly
time and eternity
transgression
translate (oneself to different
   sphere)
translating/translation (records)
tribulation
triumphant
truth
truth, rebelled against
understanding
unrighteous
valiant
vanity

vision(s)
visions, have/receive
warn/warning
warn this generation
wealth, possess (material
   possessions)
wicked/iniquitous, the
wicked, destruction of
wicked, end of
wicked (power over)
wicked conduct
wickedness
wickedness of men
wife (as companion)
wife, duties of
wife, support husband
wisdom
women, nurturing influence
women, spiritual influence
Word of the Lord, bring forth
world, the
wrongs
wrongs, to be righted
youth
Zion
Zion, city of
Zion, gathered to
Zion, inheritance in/of
Zion, land of
Zion, mountain(s) of

NOTES

PREFACE

1. Bushman (2005, 261–64).
2. Bates and Smith (2003).
3. One exception is Lavina Fielding Anderson's (2010) assessment of blessings rendered by Joseph Smith Sr., Mormonism's first patriarch.
4. See Bates (1993).
5. Berger and Luckmann (1967).

INTRODUCTION

1. In 2010 the LDS Church reported a total of 14,131,467 members worldwide. At current growth rates, approximately 1,000,000 new members are added to church rolls every two to three years. Outside the United States, LDS membership growth has been particularly notable throughout Latin America, in selected Asian countries such as the Philippines, Japan, South Korea, and Taiwan, and in African countries like Nigeria and Ghana. See Church of Jesus Christ of Latter-day Saints (2011b).

2. See Bringhurst and Foster (2008) for an in-depth account of Romney's early presidential aspirations and first attempt to gain the Republican nomination within the context of his Mormon faith. See Kranish and Hellman (2012) for what is generally conceded to be the most objective, thorough, current account of Romney's life, career, and Mormon influences.

3. *Congressional Record*, January 12, 1887, 585.

4. Mason (2011).

5. More specifically, we are employing the term "heretical" from a detached, sociological perspective that simply describes (without making a value judgment or implying a technical theological distinction) the way in which particular religious groups are, in fact, judged by majoritarian or establishment religious denominations. Thus, we apply "heretical" to religious doctrines and their corollary practices that are manifestly at variance with the authority of established orthodoxies. In sociology generally, this would be analogous to the way the concept of social "deviance" is used. Sociologists are not condemning or morally evaluating behavior that is categorized as "deviant." They are simply distinguishing behavior that is socially defined as violating the established norms of a given group from behavior that conforms with the norms of that group. Another closely parallel example would be the way that sociologists of religion employ the term "cult" in a morally neutral way, i.e., simply as a religious innovation (typically generated by the claims of a charismatic founder) that deviates markedly from already existing and socially approved religious faiths, rather than defining it as a fraudulent or criminal perversion of "true" religion. See Gary Shepherd (2007) for a discussion of these points. For sources on orthodox reactions to heresy and heretical movements in Christian history, see Christie-Murray (1989), Evans (2003), and Henderson (1998). For analyses of the tension between new religious movements and establishment religions and government agencies in American history in particular, see Davis and Hankins (2003).

6. For a summary of what social science research reveals about who joins new religions and why, see Dawson (1996).

7. Stark and Bainbridge (1985).

8. Kanter (1972).

9. For years, Rodney Stark has prominently argued that the rise and development of Mormonism constitutes the most significant contemporary case for sociological study of successful new religious movements. A compendium of his published arguments and analysis is found in Stark (2005).

10. Shepherd and Shepherd (1984, chaps. 5 and 6).

11. R. Bushman (1997, 198).

12. For studies of religious divisions that produce new religions, see J. Lewis and S. Lewis (2009).

13. Bromley (1998, 2004).

14. Shils (1965, 203).

15. Weber (1978, 1114–15).

16. The distinction between "oracular" and "inspirational" modes of prophecy, with movement from the former to the latter in Mormon history, is a theme that we expound in Shepherd and Shepherd (2009). In appendix A we offer a few examples of Joseph Smith's oracular pronouncements in contrast to subsequent statements published as revelations in the LDS Doctrine and Covenants. These comparisons illustrate the striking language differences between Smith's revelations and the declarations published by his successors in the LDS hierarchy on the momentous issues of nineteenth-century polygamy and twentieth-century priesthood eligibility for males of African descent.

Along these same lines, it is instructive to note that in 1904, when Joseph F. Smith (Joseph Smith's nephew and sixth president of the LDS Church) was being grilled under oath by Senate council during the Reed Smoot hearing, he assiduously resisted acknowledging that he had ever received any direct revelation from God binding on his co-religionists and claimed only personal inspiration with regard to matters of LDS faith. His testimony was intended to blunt charges of priestly despotism leveled against him and the LDS hierarchy. But it also was shocking for many Latter-day Saints to hear their prophet, seer, and revelator publicly disclaim the strong charisma of oracular prophecy in his tenure as church president and admit only to inspirational guidance. See Flake (2004, 76–81).

17. Wills (2007, 16).

18. The functions of "plausibility structures" for generating and sustaining different communities' worldviews are explored in Berger and Luckmann (1967).

19. For studies of belief in demonic versus angelic forces in colonial New England, see Hall (1990) and Goodbeer (1992). On the first and second Great Awakenings, see Kidd (2009), McLoughlin (1980), and Miller (1983). A general history of religion in the United States, including the religious revivals of the first and second Great Awakenings, is given in Ahlstrom (1972).

20. See especially Quinn (1998) for a definitive account of the "magical worldview" that prevailed in early nineteenth-century New York State—a worldview in which Joseph Smith and his family were avid believers and participants. See also Cross's (1950) description of religious enthusiasm in the "burned-over district" of nineteenth-century western New York.

21. For studies of Christian fundamentalism and Pentecostalism in American life, see Marsden (2006), R. Stephens (2008), and Lindsey and Silk (2005).

22. For summaries of Joseph Smith Sr.'s visionary dreams and antipathy towards sectarian religion, see R. Bushman (2005, 23–37).

23. Ibid., 199–201.

24. See Harper (2000) for a detailed discussion of some of these factors, especially the appeal of "democratic rationalism," offered by Mormon teachings to early nineteenth-century Americans. See also Moore (1986, 25–47).

25. R. Bushman (2005); Staker (2009).

26. See Bates and Smith (2003, 13–23) on the charisma and authority with which the office of LDS church patriarch was imbued.

27. Moore (1986, 5–8, 12–14, 25–30). Moore also argues that Mormons, beginning with Joseph Smith, consciously courted opposition by highlighting, and even exaggerating, the degree of their differences (31–47).

CHAPTER 1

1. Bringhurst and Hamer (2007) provide an overview of these many Mormon splinter groups.

2. Summary overviews of RLDS history from 1860 to 1990 can be found in Edwards (1991) and Howard (1992). A more recent and concise history of the Community of Christ is provided in Howlett, Hamer, and Walden (2010).

3. See Russell (2003).

4. For analysis of these and other post-1960s changes in the RLDS faith community, see Launius (1998).

5. As of 2009 there were 134 operating LDS temples worldwide, with 10 under construction and 13 more announced for construction. See Church of Jesus Christ of Latter-day Saints (2011b).

6. Russell (2008).

7. Community of Christ (2002).

8. Arrington and Bitton (1992, 16, 21). See Allen, Walker, and Whittaker (2000) for a comprehensive bibliography of nineteenth- and twentieth-century sources on Mormon history.

9. F. Turner (1921). For more recent analysis of the American frontier as the basis for cherished American myths that gloss over the grimly aggressive and violent expansionism of American frontier ideology, see Slotkin (2000). A summary conflict narrative of early Mormonism in western New York, Ohio, Missouri, and Illinois is given in chapter 2.

10. Shipps (1998, 81–109).

11. For analyses of events preceding and following the military occupation of Salt Lake City in the "Utah War" of 1857–58, see Arrington and Walker (2004), Furniss (1960), and MacKinnon (2008). Gordon (2001) provides a historical analysis of the legal issues involved in the Mormons' ultimately lost struggle to defend the practice of polygamy in nineteenth-century America. See also Flake's (2004) study of the ultimate legal and political reconciliation of the LDS Church with national institutions as a result of Senate investigative hearings from 1903 to 1907 on the question of Mormon apostle Reed Smoot's fitness to take his seat as Utah senator, in the process of which virtually every aspect of Mormonism's theocratic religious culture was reproachfully examined.

12. For studies of Mormonism's transformation from despised nineteenth-century sect to twentieth-century respectability and international expansion, see Alexander (1996); Gottlieb and Wiley (1984); Mauss (1994); Ostling and Ostling (2000); Quinn (1997); Shepherd and Shepherd (1984); Stark (2005); and O'Dea (1957).

13. In 2010 the LDS Church reported totals of 340 missions (designated areas of organized proselytizing activity), 17 missionary training centers, and 52,814 full-time missionaries worldwide (Church of Jesus Christ of Latter-day Saints [2011b]). At the same time, a major concern for contemporary LDS officials is the rate at which converts

added to church rolls through extensive missionary efforts quickly drop out or fail to become "active" members (the *sine qua non* of the Mormon lay religion). Thus, modern Mormonism's rapid worldwide growth must be considered relative to how many of its convert baptisms actually produce committed new members. Available statistics show a substantial gap between reported convert baptisms and active, participating members. Consequently, LDS missionary priorities have begun shifting from sheer membership growth objectives to greater selectivity in convert recruitment and retention. See the Church of Jesus Christ of Latter-day Saints *Ensign* magazine (2007). For scholarly analyses, see Cragun and Lawson (2010), Phillips (2006; 2008), Shepherd and Shepherd (1996), and Stewart (2007).

14. For a large-scale analysis of the rise of individualism at the expense of community commitment in American culture, see Bellah et al. (2007). At the same time, building or revitalizing member commitment is a major concern in contemporary religious communities. The following books address this concern in American Protestant, Catholic, and Jewish faiths, respectively: Roof (1983), Schneiders (2001), and Eisen (2000). For historical comparisons and theoretical analysis of commitment in nineteenth-century versus twentieth-century American communal groups, see Kanter (1972).

15. Among his first blessings as church patriarch, to his sons Joseph Jr. and Hyrum, Father Smith asserted the Latter-day Saints' kinship with the ancient Hebrew patriarchs and his sons' preordained latter-day roles in the restoration of the House of Israel to be gathered to a new land of Zion. To Joseph Jr. he declared, "Thou hast been called, even in thy youth to the great work of the Lord . . . even that which shall prepare the way for the remnants of his people to come in among the gentiles, with their fullness, as the tribes of Israel are restored. I bless thee with the blessings of thy fathers Abraham, Isaac and Jacob . . . my seed are to inherit the choice land whereon the Zion of God shall stand in the last days, from among my seed, scattered with the gentiles, shall a choice seer arise . . . whose mouth shall utter the law of the just" (Marquardt 2007, 14). To Hyrum he said, "I now ask my heavenly Father in the name of Jesus Christ to bless thee with the same blessings with which Jacob blessed his son Joseph, for thou art his true descendant, and thy posterity shall be numbered with the house of Ephraim, and with them thou shalt stand up to crown the tribes of Israel, when they come shouting to Zion" (ibid., 12). For an in-depth examination of LDS beliefs concerning their Hebraic lineage, see Mauss (2003).

16. R. Bushman (2005, 262–63).

17. The latent functions of human institutions are analyzed and discussed in Merton (1968).

18. Kanter (1972).

19. Shepherd and Shepherd (1984).

20. Stark (1999, 287).

21. Arguably, the two most compelling and influential biographies of Joseph Smith published over the past sixty-five years are authored by Brodie (1945) and R. Bushman (2005). While their underlying assumptions concerning the ultimate authenticity of Smith's prophetic claims are diametrically opposed, both Brodie and Bushman portray Smith as a complex and creative personality who simultaneously developed organizational and leadership skills as he matured and was significantly influenced by those whom he designated for high office in the church hierarchy.

22. Neilson and Givens (2008, 7).

23. See, for example, Harper (2009), Staker (2009), and Underwood (2009), all of whom emphasize the interactive development of early Mormon teachings.

24. For a theoretical exposition of the differences between traditional, legal, and charismatic forms of authority and the historical transformation of the latter into the former, see Weber (1978, 246–71, 1111–57).

25. O'Dea (1961).

26. See Bebbington (1989), Hughes (1988), Hughes and Allen (2000), and Sandeen (1978).

27. For studies of early nineteenth-century enthusiasm for spiritual renewal in general and the appeal to early LDS converts of Christian "primitivism" in particular, see Hill (1968), Cross (1950), Rust (2004), Vogel (1988), and Underwood (1993).

28. In his research on revivals in western New York during the 1820s, Quinn (2006) documents Methodist camp revivals that attracted as many as 20,000 frontier New Yorkers to virtual tent cities erected in forested clearings for days of spiritual regeneration and conversion.

29. Quinn (1994).

30. On the role played by the Book of Mormon in early LDS recruiting success, see Givens (2002). See also R. Bushman (2005), Harper (2000), Hansen (1970), O'Dea (1957), and Shipps (1985). Critical or debunking assessments of the historicity of the Book of Mormon can be found in Vogel and Metcalfe (2002).

31. Neilson and Givens (2008).

32. R. Bushman (2005, 131–42).

33. Shipps (1985, 67–85).

34. Joseph Smith's most important organizational and doctrinal revelations have been canonized by the LDS Church in the Doctrine and Covenants. Facsimiles of Joseph Smith's early (1832–39) written and/or dictated journals, revelations, and translations are reproduced and published in Jessee, Esplin, and Bushman (2008; 2009).

35. On the importance of primary group social networks in the emergence of new prophetic religions, see Stark (1999); see also Dawson (2008) on the formation of new religious movements.

36. For biographical accounts of some of these influential early converts, see Welch (2006), Pratt (2000), Van Wagoner (1994), and Brown (2008).

37. See Underwood (2009); see also Harper (2009).

38. The seventh article in the LDS Church's Articles of Faith, as summarized by Joseph Smith to the *Chicago Democrat* in 1842, states, "We believe in the gift of tongues, prophecy, revelation, visions, healing, interpretation of tongues, and so forth." For historical commentary on Mormonism's articles of faith, see Whittaker (1987). While extravagant display of "spiritual gifts" in the mode of revival camp meetings was usually avoided in early LDS Church meetings after Joseph Smith arrived in Kirtland to preside over his rapidly expanding flock, speaking in tongues was not an uncommon practice, and both men and women participated in the highly ecstatic 1836 dedication of the Kirtland Temple. Miraculous healings were commonly reported throughout this period and well beyond. For a review of nineteenth-century LDS women's practice of spiritual gifts in particular, see Newell (1987).

39. Joseph's oldest brother, Alvin, suffered a premature death in 1823 at the age of twenty-five. Davies (2000, 86ff., 98ff.) argues that this traumatic loss had a significant impact on Joseph Smith's later innovative teachings concerning "baptism for the dead" and ultimate human salvation, which are further discussed in chapter 5.

40. R. Bushman (2005, 261–63); see also Stark (1999).

41. Bates and Smith (2003, 35–36). Prior to his ordination as church patriarch, Father Smith was ordained as a high priest in 1831, and in 1837 he was sustained as assistant counselor to the First Presidency.

42. Mauss (2003, 17–14); Quinn (2009).

CHAPTER 2

1. Stark (1999); Dawson (2008, 39–70).

2. Quinn (1998, 2006).

3. Major historical sources that we consulted for our narrative synopsis of early Mormon history in New York include Brodie (1945), R. Bushman (1984; 2005), Marquardt and Walters (1998), and Quinn (1998).

4. L. Smith (2007).

5. After the death of his oldest brother, Alvin, in 1823, Joseph developed a particularly close relationship with his brother Hyrum, who thereafter assumed the role of elder sibling and loyal counselor.

6. Scholarly debates concerning the accuracy of Smith's several accounts of his early religious experiences can be found in Hill (2001), Quinn (2006), Marquardt and Walters (1998), and Vogel (1996).

7. "Transcription" is the term suggested by R. Bushman (2005, 72–73), in lieu of either "translation," as conventionally understood, or "composition," to denote the process by which Joseph Smith produced the Book of Mormon.

8. Biographical essays on Oliver Cowdery can be found in Welch (2006).

9. Good historical sources on early Mormonism in Ohio include Backman (1983), Robison (1997), and especially Staker (2009).

10. Doctrine and Covenants 38:32.

11. Doctrine and Covenants 1:1, 8.

12. L. Anderson (2010, 1).

13. Staker (2009, 345).

14. Ibid., 319–28. Interestingly, heated doctrinal controversy has again flared in contemporary evangelical circles over the traditionally bifurcated view of heaven and hell in Rob Bell's book, *Love Wins: A Book About Heaven, Hell, and the Fate of Every Person Who Ever Lived* (2011).

15. In Max Weber's analysis of charisma, the enduring mark of charismatic leadership rests not in the ability to make convincing supernatural claims about one's station or calling, but in the innovative ability to meet real tests and demonstrate self-confidence and resolve in a crisis (1978, 1111–12). Joseph Smith's handling of the Missouri crisis and its aftermath illustrates this kind of charisma.

16. R. Bushman (2005, 319).

17. McGrane (1965).

18. Staker (2009, 536).

19. Ibid., 551.

20. Historical sources for understanding early Mormonism in Missouri include Kinney (2011), Lesueur (1987), and Spencer (2010).

21. Van Wagoner (1994, 218).

22. Roberts (1978, 190–91).

23. Scholarly sources detailing early Mormon history in Illinois include Flanders (1965) and G. Leonard (2002).

24. R. Bushman (2005, 382).

25. Roberts (1965, 11).

26. Bates and Smith (2003, 50).

27. At the 1840 April Conference, an oracular-voiced revelation, subsequently published in the Doctrine and Covenants (124:91–95), was read to the conference confirming Hyrum's rightful ascension to the office of church patriarch and acknowledging his standing next to that of the prophet: "that my servant Hyrum may take the office of Priesthood and Patriarch, which was appointed unto him by his father, by blessing and also by right; That from henceforth he shall hold the patriarchal blessings upon the heads of all my people, that whatsoever he blesses shall be blessed, and whosoever he curses shall be cursed: that whatsoever he shall bind on earth shall be bound in heaven . . . and from this time forth I appoint unto him that he may be a prophet, and a seer, and a revelator unto my church, as well as my servant Joseph; that he may act in concert

also with my servant Joseph and that he shall receive counsel from my servant Joseph, who shall show unto him the keys whereby he may ask and receive, and be crowned with the same blessing, and honor, and priesthood, and gifts of the priesthood that once were put upon him that was my servant Oliver Cowdery."

28. For a complete account of Bennett's astounding career as a con artist *par excellence*, including his fateful entanglements with Joseph Smith and the Mormons in Nauvoo, see A. Smith (1997).

29. Bennett, Black, and Cannon (2010, 77–125).

30. For Smith's official revelation on plural marriage, see Doctrine and Covenants 132:239–245.

31. Compton (1997) meticulously documents the thirty-three women who, over the space of a dozen years, Smith claimed as plural wives.

32. LDS stakes are ecclesiastical units analogous to Catholic dioceses.

33. Roberts (1978, 302–17). Among other things, in his address Smith discoursed on the eternal plurality of gods, outlining a theology of deification in which the human race, through obedience to the principles of the restored gospel, might advance in knowledge, power, and perfection to become celestialized gods and rulers in the timeless beyond. Further discussion of this doctrine is reviewed, along with LDS salvation theology, in chapter 5.

34. Roberts (1965, 413).

35. See Bates (1983) and Edwards (1985) for summaries of William Smith's contentious relationship with Brigham Young and the apostles, his removal from office, and his unsuccessful efforts to reclaim what he continued to assert was his rightful station in the RLDS restoration movement.

36. For sources on the Mormons' migration to the Rocky Mountains and their colonization of the Utah Territory, see Arrington (1986), Arrington and Walker (2004), and Stegner (1992).

37. See James B. Allen (2002) for the life and times of William Clayton.

38. Ibid.

CHAPTER 3

1. R. Bushman (2005, 261).

2. Bates and Smith (2003, 50).

3. Bates and Smith (2003, 32) give the date of Father Smith's patriarchal ordination as December 18, 1833. While conceding historical ambiguity, Marquardt (2007, ix) offers circumstantial evidence that the ordination occurred on or around December 6, 1834.

4. Bates and Smith (2003, 33–34). The only instance of "local" patriarchs being called to officiate in this office during the time period of our study was in England during an extremely productive missionary campaign led by the Quorum of the Twelve Apostles in 1840–41. Joseph Smith had previously instructed the apostles that "an Evangelist is a Patriarch, even the oldest man of the blood of Joseph or of the seed of Abraham. Wherever the church is established in the earth, there should be a Patriarch for benefiting the posterity of the Saints" (ibid., 47). Several thousand Mormon converts were living in England at this time without this benefit. Accordingly, Heber C. Kimball and Brigham Young, respectively, nominated two qualified English converts to serve as patriarchs for England: Peter Melling and John Albiston, each of whom subsequently issued blessings to British members following the format established by Joseph Smith and his father. Prior to the ordination of Melling and Albiston, the apostles themselves occasionally gave patriarchal blessings to British members. See Allen (2002), 19.

5. As indicated in chapter 2, relations between William and his fellow members of the Twelve, especially Brigham Young, were badly strained, and within four months of his succession as church patriarch in May 1845, the apostles moved to have William removed from the Quorum, stripped of his patriarchal office, and excommunicated from the church on grounds of apostasy.

6. R. Bushman (2005, 262–63). A hagiographic bibliography of Smith Sr. with numerous anecdotal details is rendered by Earnest Skinner (2002).

7. Marquardt (2007, 65).

8. Ibid., 69.

9. Ibid., 154.

10. Ibid., 177.

11. *Informal* rituals enacted in face-to-face encounters in daily life are analyzed by Goffman (1967).

12. Terrin (2007, 3933).

13. For an interdisciplinary set of readings on the variegated characteristics of human ritual, see Grimes (1995). Also see Davies (2002, 111–16) for a specific focus on analytical assumptions regarding religious rituals.

14. As pointed out by Bates and Smith (2003, 49), "In many of the Patriarch's blessings he uses the phrase 'I seal you up unto eternal life.' At the time the 'sealing power' was associated with the High Priesthood [i.e., Melchizedek Priesthood]. . . . Elders who were members of the High Priesthood used this sealing power in the early 1830s. . . . The sealing power of the patriarchate became of record in 1841 with the revelation set forth in Doctrine and Covenants 124:93 and 124."

15. The manner in which LDS patriarchal blessings are bestowed is briefly described in Ballif (1992).

16. See Wuthnow (2011) for a discussion of the social science significance of qualitative analysis of religious "talk"—the religious language used by believers. We concur with Wuthnow's emphasis on the importance of language in understanding religious practice. Our content analysis of patriarchal blessings directly testifies to this importance. Even though our overt method of analysis is quantitative, our final interpretation of statistical findings relies on a qualitative understanding of Mormon meanings in the context of Mormon history and culture.

17. The social psychological notion of religious compensators is formally spelled out by Stark and Bainbridge in their influential article "Towards a Theory of Religion: Religious Commitment" (1979). In brief, Stark and Bainbridge regard religious organizations as systems that specialize in general, supernaturally-based "compensators." Compensators are defined as "intangible substitutes" for rewards that cannot be unequivocally demonstrated but are nevertheless highly valued. Thus, "compensators function *as if* they were rewards," and religious adherents are willing "to expend costs to obtain them." Employing Stark and Bainbridge's language, the contingent promises contained in patriarchal blessings may be described as conferring supernatural compensators to blessing recipients in exchange for their faithful commitment to the teachings of the restored gospel and loyal obedience to LDS priesthood authority.

It should also be noted that ritual practices are often polysemic in their social and psychological consequences—that is, they may be understood as serving multiple interrelated functions. Thus, in addition to their compensatory commitment function, solidarity and doctrinal functions may also be attributed to patriarchal blessings, as we emphasize in the remainder of this chapter.

18. While patriarchal blessings are unique in their particulars, other religious faith traditions also offer ritualized, albeit much more generic, blessings to their communicants. See Balentine (1993), Jungmann (2008), and Lindgren (2005). Likewise, statements included in patriarchal blessings concerning blessing recipients' character and

future prospects are superficially similar to "readings" given by astrologers, numerologists, spiritualist mediums, and other kinds of "diviners." But even if electronically recorded, relatively few of these kinds of pronouncements are routinely transcribed and given to recipients as sacred artifacts to treasure and preserve, as is the case with Mormon blessing recipients. See T. Leonard (2005).

19. L. Anderson (2010, 14).

20. Staker (2009, 244–45). For documented references to other blessing meetings in Kirtland, see Bates and Smith (2003, 38–39, 44, 48–49).

21. Bates and Smith (2003, 43).

22. L. Anderson (2010, 14).

23. Ibid., 88.

24. Ibid., 44.

25. Ibid., 84.

26. Ibid., 94.

27. L. Anderson (2010).

28. Bates and Smith (2003, 38).

29. Ibid., 160.

30. Shipps (1985).

31. Quinn (2009).

32. Shipps (1998, 83).

33. A careful textual analysis of the development of early LDS priesthood doctrines can be found in Prince (1995).

34. In his 1838 personal history (elaborating on his earlier 1830 and 1832 accounts), Joseph Smith gave the date of John the Baptist's visitation, returning to earth as a celestialized being, as May 15, 1829. See Roberts (1978, 39–41). In 1830 Smith avowed that he and Cowdery had received the Melchizedek Priesthood and been ordained to the apostleship by Peter, James, and John—also now celestialized beings—but gave no specific date for this event, which putatively occurred in May 1829 subsequent to the restoration of the Aaronic Priesthood through John the Baptist. See Doctrine and Covenants 27:12.

35. On LDS covenant making, see Cooper (1990).

36. See Mauss (2003) for the definitive discussion of these beliefs and their wide-ranging implications and consequences for modern Mormonism.

37. See Doctrine and Covenants 6:3, 50:2. For commentary and exposition by one of Hyrum Smith's grandsons (and tenth president of the LDS Church), see J. Smith (1945); see also Harper (2008).

38. For a historical account of the institution of plural marriage, see Van Wagoner (1989).

39. For a chronological analysis of the development and adaptive change of LDS temple practices in conjunction with other developments in Mormon history, see D. Anderson (2010) and Buerger (2002).

40. Doctrine and Covenants 132:7. This disquisition on priesthood sealing power was prefatory to the lengthy revelation Joseph Smith announced in justification of the doctrine and practice of plural marriage; see the remainder of Doctrine and Covenants 132:15–66.

41. Marquardt (2007, 68). Charles C. Rich was an early Mormon convert (1831) who subsequently, in 1849, was called by Brigham Young to become a member of the Quorum of the Twelve Apostles.

42. Ibid., 205–6. Biographical information on Susanna White does not appear to exist beyond this recorded blessing, which identifies her as a probable British convert and a member of the church in good standing at that time.

43. Ibid., 366–67. Levi Runyan was a relatively new Mormon convert at the time of his blessing. He subsequently joined the Mormon flight from Nauvoo, Illinois, in early 1846 and, while en route with those refugees who followed the leadership of Brigham Young, was among the five hundred men recruited by the U.S. Army in 1847 to serve in the short-lived Mexican War as a member of the "Mormon Battalion."

CHAPTER 4

1. Marquardt (2007, x).

2. In Utah the office of church historian and recorder was singled out as an official priesthood calling whose duties typically have been discharged by designated apostles or other LDS general authorities. See Bitton and Arrington (1988) and Searle (1992).

3. Men named in Marquardt's compilation as both clerk and recorder: Oliver Cowdery and George W. Robinson. Men named as clerks only: W. E. McLellin, T. B. Marsh, F. G.Williams, W. W. Phelps, G. W. Robinson, John Whitmer, E. M. Greene, Sylvester Smith, S. W. Denton, E. Wightman, S. James, H. Clark, E. Robinson, L. Davis, J. Sloan, and H. Coray. Men named as scribes: Sylvester Smith, S. W. Knapps, J. Gould, J. Pine, L. M. Smith, W. Woodruff, F. G. Williams, H. Clark, E. D. Woolley, J. C. Snow, Z. H. Gurley, and R. B. Thompson. Men named as recorders: O. Cowdery, W. A. Cowdery, Sylvester Smith, W. Richards, and R. Campbell.

4. Bates and Smith (2003, 52n23); Marquardt (2007, x).

5. We do not know exactly when the sound recording of patriarchal blessings became standard LDS practice, but reel-to-reel tape recorders were commercially available for personal use by the mid-1950s. We know from personal experience that blessings were being sound-recorded by stake patriarchs by at least the early 1960s.

6. See, for example, Ehrman (2007a; 2007b).

7. Marquardt (2007, ix).

8. Bates (1993).

9. Marquardt (2007, vii).

10. Ibid., 4–10.

11. Ibid., 49–55, 216.

12. In none of his blessings to family members did Joseph Jr. specify their lineal, tribal descent from the House of Israel. He did, however, expressly link Joseph Sr.'s restored office and authority with that of Adam—the "Ancient of Days"—and subsequent Old Testament patriarchs of Adam's posterity, and also with the "mighty God of Jacob, and the God of his Fathers; Even the God of Abraham, Isaac and Jacob" (Marquardt 2007, 4). In blessing Hyrum, he subsequently declared that Hyrum stood "in the tracks of his father" and was "numbered among those who hold the right of patriarchal priesthood" (ibid., 5), simultaneously affirming the Latter-day Saints' Hebraic priesthood affinity and implying the hereditary character of the office of church patriarch. The ultra-supernatural foundations of LDS restoration theology are also vividly expressed in Joseph Jr.'s blessing of his father: "while the visions of the Almighty were open to his view, saying: 'Three years previous to the death of Adam, he called Seth, Enos, Cainan, Mahalaleel, Jared, Enoch, and Methuselah, who were high priests, with the residue of his posterity, who were righteous into the valley of Adamondi-ahman, and there bestowed upon them his last blessing. And the Lord appeared unto them, and they rose up and blessed Adam, and called him Michael the Prince, the Archangel. . . . So shall it be with my father: he shall be called a prince over his posterity, holding the keys of the patriarchal priesthood over the Kingdom of God, even the Church of the Latter Day Saints, and he shall sit in the general assembly of patriarchs, even in council with the Ancient of Days when he shall sit and all the patriarch with

him—and shall enjoy his right and authority under the direction of the Ancient of Days'" (ibid., 4).

13. For analyses of William's brief and controversial tenure as church patriarch, see Bates (1983) and Edwards (1985).

14. Our method for randomly selecting 15 male and 15 female blessings from each patriarch's total was to separate blessings for males and females into gender subsets, count the number of blessings for each sex, then divide that number by 15. The quotient told us how many blessings to skip from the selection of one case to the next for a particular patriarch's subset of blessings according to gender. For example, in Marquardt's compilation of Joseph Sr.'s blessings, 151 were for females and 222 were for males. Dividing 151 female blessings by 15 gave us every tenth case in Joseph Sr.'s subset of female blessings, while dividing 222 by 15 gave us every fifteenth case in the selection of male blessings. For Hyrum's set of 64 blessings, we selected every other case from the subsets of both sexes, and for William's set of 300 blessings, we selected every tenth case from the subsets of both sexes. The blessings drawn into our sample are listed in appendix B.

15. Our thematic word index is given in appendix C.

16. Our content analysis method for assessing patriarchal blessing themes was similar to the one we employed in an earlier study of LDS general conference addresses. See Shepherd and Shepherd (1984).

17. The SPSS (Statistical Package for the Social Sciences) software processes quantitative data sets and calculates a wide variety of statistical measures.

CHAPTER 5

1. The polemics by Bennett (1999), Larsen (2008), and Tucker (1989) are illustrative. For an apologetic LDS analysis of the "social construction" of Mormon heresy, see Givens (1997).

2. R. Bushman (2005, 195–202).

3. The Mormon idiomatic usage of "exaltation" is employed by current LDS authorities and lay members in talks and articles to denote the ultimate purpose of human existence. In Mormonism, exaltation specifies the meaning of Christian salvation and eternal life for individuals who accept and obey the requirements of the restored gospel by signifying a deified status in God's celestial kingdom in which family and marital relationships are eternally sustained and augmented. During the first several decades of the Mormon restoration, however, the term "exaltation" does not appear to have been commonly used. It was not coded, for example, in any of the ninety blessings we sampled from Marquardt's compilation. In those blessings, the analogous and more familiar soteriological terms "salvation," "eternal life," "celestial glory," and so on were used instead of "exaltation." Joseph Smith himself only sparingly employed the word "exaltation" in his official revelations published in the Doctrine and Covenants, most notably in his 1843 revelation of the "new and everlasting covenant" of celestial marriage, published less than a year prior to his 1844 assassination (see Doctrine and Covenants 132). (Smith's revelation on celestial marriage specifically affirmed divine sanction of plural marriage, for which he took pains to provide a lengthy theological rationale.) At the same time, corresponding soteriological terms such as "celestial glory," "eternity," "eternal life," "heaven," "salvation," "sanctification," and the like are widely distributed throughout the various verses of Joseph Smith's revelations recorded elsewhere in the Doctrine and Covenants. From its relative absence in documents recorded prior to the Mormon hegira to the Rocky Mountains in 1846–47, we infer that the term "exaltation" was popularized by subsequent generations of LDS officials and theologians as a way

of codifying the most important aspect of Mormon salvation theology that emerged in Nauvoo before Smith's death, including plural marriage.

This inference is supported by data we obtained from an earlier study of LDS conference reports (see Shepherd and Shepherd 1984). During Mormonism's first generation (1830–59), the term "exaltation" appeared in only a few conference talks delivered by LDS general authorities in the Utah Territory. A generation later (1860–89), following the official acknowledgment and vigorous theological defense of plural marriage by Utah Mormons, conference references to exaltation were three times more frequent. By Mormonism's third generation (1890–1919), conference references to exaltation peaked at a frequency rate that was eleven times greater than in first-generation conference sermons. It was notably in 1890—at the onset of Mormonism's third generation— that the practice of plural marriage was first officially abjured. Thereafter, Mormon theologians and church authorities speaking at general conference have expounded the doctrine of eternal exaltation through *monogamous* marriages performed in LDS temples by the sealing power of the restored priesthood. And, in recent decades, they have downplayed the radical implications of human deification, instead emphasizing the corporate salvation of the nuclear family as an eternal unit in the celestial kingdom.

For a good example of how these themes are currently taught in the LDS Church, see Apostle Dallin H. Oaks's (2010) talk to the Harvard Law School, "Fundamental Premises of our Faith," in which he says, "Our theology begins with the assurance that we lived as spirits before we came to this earth. It affirms that this mortal life has a purpose. And it teaches that our highest aspiration is to become like our Heavenly Parents, which will empower us to perpetuate our family relationships throughout eternity. We were placed here on earth to acquire a physical body and, through the atonement of Jesus Christ and by obedience to the laws and ordinances of His gospel, to qualify for the glorified celestial condition and relationships that are called exaltation or eternal life. . . . For us, 'eternal life' in the celestial, the highest of these glories, is not a mystical union with an incomprehensible spirit-god. As noted earlier, eternal life is family life with a loving Father in Heaven and with our progenitors and our posterity."

Finally, we should also note that the LDS concept of exaltation and its attendant implications for ultimate human deification were, along with plural marriage, repudiated by the RLDS Church in the nineteenth century. Consequently, it is not a term employed by current Community of Christ leaders.

4. McMurrin (1965, 83). Adherence to Mormon salvation doctrine by the modern LDS Church's most devout members underlies their tireless commitment to missionary proselytizing, genealogical research, and participation in the performance of temple ordinances, including baptism for the dead, obtaining one's personal endowment, and contracting monogamous marriages for time and eternity—all of which we review further in the concluding chapter. Mormonism's renowned work ethic is theologically linked to its distinctive doctrines of salvation, which require not only assent to and grateful acknowledgment of God's grace, but also the active commitment of Latter-day Saints to the religious programs of their church in order to realize God's ultimate plans for his spiritual offspring. For an extended exposition of the link between Mormon soteriological beliefs and energized religious activity as the LDS norm, see Davies (2000).

5. On occasion, William's volatile temper prompted open conflicts with his brother Joseph—including shouting matches and at least one violent physical confrontation. See R. Bushman (2005, 299–302).

6. Ibid., 54–55; see also Stark (1999, 297–98).

7. For a historical exposition and analysis of LDS temple worship, see Buerger (2002). The Mormons were driven out of Missouri before they could marshal the necessary resources to construct temples in Independence or Far West. In Nauvoo, the apostles made completion of the temple a priority task after the assassinations of Joseph

and Hyrum, so that church members could receive temple endowments prior to embarking on their evacuation of the city. Upon reaching the desolate valley of the Great Salt Lake, Brigham Young and the vanguard company virtually made it their first order of business to stake out consecrated grounds for construction of the Salt Lake Temple. By dint of their exclusion of outside observers, LDS temple ceremonies, both in Nauvoo and later in Utah, contrasted with the quasi-public character of patriarchal blessings, which often were bestowed on multiple recipients as a form of community worship. In the concluding chapter we consider the ascendant commitment function of temple participation relative to the administration of patriarchal blessings in the contemporary LDS Church.

8. Quinn (2009). See also Erickson (1975), Nibley (1989), and Underwood (1993).

9. Hansen (1970); see also Quinn (1980).

10. Describing the Holy Ghost as a distinctive material being would appear to be a contradiction in terms. But in Joseph Smith's metaphysics, the orthodox distinction between matter and spirit is viewed as a false dichotomy. With regard to the resurrection of the body, Smith taught that both "the spirit and the body are the soul of man" (Doctrine and Covenants 88:1), and though separated at death, they will be permanently reunited in the resurrection. He declared, "There is no such thing as immaterial matter. All spirit is matter, but it is more fine or pure, and can only be discerned by purer eyes; we cannot see it; but when our bodies are purified we shall see that it is all matter" (Doctrine and Covenants 131:7–8). Thus it may be said that, consistent with its supernatural literalism, Mormon doctrine materializes the spiritual while spiritualizing the material. In this theological formulation it is not contradictory to say that the Holy Ghost—a spiritual entity—also possesses material being. Whether or not at some future time, the Holy Ghost is destined to obtain a "glorified" body like those imputed to the "Father and the Son" is an open theological question not stipulated in Mormon scripture. For the materialistic aspects of Mormon theology and its practical implications for Mormonism as a way of life, see Shepherd and Shepherd (1984, 56–59).

11. For a description of both the dogged devotion and painful travails of the Mormon handcart companies in particular, see Stegner (1992).

CHAPTER 6

1. Durkheim (1968).

2. Ibid. Besides Durkheim, other functionalist theorists emphasizing links between ritual and social solidarity are discussed in Alexander and Smith (2005). See in particular V. Turner (1995). The view that rituals reinforce structures of domination is expressed in Lukes (1975), Foucault (1995), and Kertzer (1989). Ritual as a means for grassroots contestation and mobilization is explored in Collins (2005).

3. In 1978 the LDS priesthood ban on ordaining males of African descent was lifted through an official declaration of the First Presidency. For subsequent commentary by Mormon scholars, see Bush and Mauss (1984); see also Bringhurst and Smith (2006). Meanwhile, LDS women remain ineligible for ordination to the Aaronic or governing Melchizedek orders of the priesthood, which continue to be male prerogatives. At the same time, LDS authorities continue to emphasize that women *share* with their husbands the "patriarchal order of the priesthood" through their temple marriage covenant, which also seals both parents to their children and their children's children in one eternal family unit. See McKinlay (1992, 1067).

4. I. Lewis (2003).

5. Bates and Smith (2003, 55n53) quote from the recollections of a Kirtland member: "In the summer of 1834, Father Joseph Smith, Sr., commenced to visit the families

of the Saints and give patriarchal blessings, and greatly was the Spirit of the Lord manifested among the Saints in the gift of tongues, with interpretation, prophecy, and the gift of healing."

6. For an overview and synthesis of scholarship from a wide range of interdisciplinary studies on women in nineteenth-century America, see Clinton and Lunardini (2006). A comprehensive historical narrative of women's changing roles and contributions to American history is provided in Dubois and Dumenil (2005). See also an earlier classic study by Hartman and Banner (1974).

7. The notion of "republican motherhood" is described by Kerber (1997); see also Norton (1980). For an analysis of the increasingly dominant role played by women in the American temperance movement, see Fletcher (2007) and Parsons (2003). For summaries of scholarship on women's nineteenth-century efforts to achieve political suffrage and reproductive control, see Clinton and Lunardini (2006).

8. A small sampling of Mormon feminist scholarship would include Anderson and Bates (2001); Beecher and Anderson (1987); Bradley (2005); C. Bushman (1997); Cornwall (1994); Derr, Cannon, and Beecher (1992); Foster (1979); Hanks (1992); Iannaccone and Miles (1994); and Newell and Avery (1994).

9. The contrast between the relatively liberating aspects of nineteenth-century Mormonism for women and its subsequent conservative turn is reflected in the essays published in Beecher and Anderson (1987). See also Bradley (1994). The view that contemporary LDS women's lives are systematically suppressed by LDS patriarchal institutions is emphatically expressed by Johnson (1981) and Warenski (1978).

10. See Welter (1966; 1985); see also Mathews (1987).

11. For discussions of the strains produced by a traditional view of women and women's family roles in the contemporary LDS Church, see articles by Bennion (2008) and Miles (2008).

12. When patriarchal blessings were first instituted, minor children as well as adults were given blessings. Thus, in our coding of Marquardt's compilation, the ages of blessing recipients ranged from 1 to 85 years of age. However, only seventeen recipients were 12 or younger, while the largest age cohort consisted of individuals who were ages 20 to 29, representing over one-third of blessing recipients in the compilation. These figures remind us that Mormonism, like most new religious movements, tended to attract young adults. Joseph Smith himself was only 25 years old when he organized the Church of Christ in 1830.

13. We used Pearson's chi-square tests for calculating the significance of thematic frequency differences between male and female blessings.

14. Today, young women, as well as married couples, serve proselytizing missions for the LDS Church. At the same time, missionary work is still considered to be a priesthood responsibility incumbent on young men but optional for young women. For an analysis of LDS missionary callings as a male rite of passage, see Shepherd and Shepherd (1998, 21–29).

15. R. Bushman (2005, 263). The following sources provide analyses of the Latter-day Saints' conception of Zion as both a material and spiritual community, operationally linked with the "United Order" as a cooperative economic program for realizing the Kingdom of God on earth: Arrington, Fox, and May (1976); Arrington and Walker (2004); and Geddes (1922).

16. Legal histories of the gradual change of property law in both the American colonial period and the nineteenth century with respect to women's rights can be found in Salmon (1989) and Hartog (2000).

17. See Newell and Avery (1994). For a comprehensive study of women's nineteenth-century health issues, see Leavitt (1999).

18. Mauss (2003) has analyzed the latent consequences of Old Testament lineage claims for the ethnocentric construction of LDS racial identities. As Mauss argues, these initial exclusionary boundaries have gradually broadened in the twentieth and twenty-first centuries as a result of massive missionary efforts and worldwide expansion.

19. For an analysis of the group commitment functions of transcendent beliefs that justify mortification and personal suffering, see Kanter (1972, 111–25).

20. See the essays published in Beecher and Anderson (1987) and Hanks (1992), especially Quinn's (1992) essay "Mormon Women Have Had the Priesthood Since 1843."

21. It might be counter-argued that, regardless of relative gender balance in their ideational contents, patriarchal blessings are an inherently latent device for ultimately reinforcing women's false consciousness in embracing a religious way of life that subverts their interests by subordinating them to the administrative control of men. In this regard it is instructive to recall that, in contrast to the LDS Church's current social conservatism, the more liberal Community of Christ (formerly the RLDS Church) ordains women as well as men to priesthood offices, including the equivalent of LDS patriarchs, who administer the equivalent of LDS patriarchal blessings. Significantly, however, the explicitly male designations of "patriarch" and "patriarchal" have been replaced by the gender-neutral terms of "evangelist" and "evangelical." Thus, in the Community of Christ, patriarchal blessings are now called "evangelist's blessings" and are bestowed by ordained "ministers of blessing" on anyone—including nonmembers—over the age of eight who requests a blessing. For a historical overview of patriarchal blessings as understood and practiced by the Community of Christ, see Howard (2010).

22. Shipps (1987, ix).

23. Ibid., vii–ix.

24. The generally conservative views and administrative decisions formulated by key general authorities positioned in the Mormon hierarchy throughout the twentieth century—particularly members of the Quorum of the Twelve and First Presidency—are documented in Quinn (1997). Focusing on women's' issues in particular, the transformation of a once-radical religion into a bastion of social conservatism is documented in Bradley's (2005) balanced analysis of the active role played by the LDS Church in marshaling opposition to passage of the ERA amendment to the U.S. Constitution.

25. As Bates (1993, 2) points out, in contrast to the more open character of nineteenth-century patriarchal blessings, scholarly access to contemporary blessings is often difficult: "With the current official emphasis on the privacy of patriarchal blessings many members are reluctant to share them." In conjunction with the privatization of patriarchal blessings, the very large number of blessings currently given annually by thousands of different stake patriarchs worldwide makes the possibility of obtaining a truly representative sample of contemporary LDS patriarchal blessings a daunting task.

CHAPTER 7

1. Bates and Smith (2003).

2. Flake (2004, 8).

3. Ibid., 82–108. These official church reversals of nineteenth-century LDS commitment to the practice of plural marriage led to the reactionary formation of various Mormon splinter groups, whose descendants continue to practice plural marriage and consider themselves to be the true disciples of the new and everlasting covenant. For a wide-ranging set of essays on the history, religious culture, and legal issues of these

groups, see Jacobson and Burton (2011). See also Hardy (2011) for an extensive examination of the remarkable persistence of Mormon polygamy.

4. In his analysis of religious activity in contemporary LDS culture, Sorenson (2000, 121) argues that "ritual behavior in these activities pervades Mormon life." Sorenson identifies a large, but not inclusive, number of religiously directed LDS behaviors that he categorizes under different ritual dimensions, involving (1) the social scale of participation (from individuals to families to various congregational levels), and (2) a religious scale indicating the degree to which LDS doctrinal beliefs dominate the action. His religious-scale categories include patently religious rituals, substantially religious rituals (despite other concerns), and social rituals (with significant religious involvement or overtones). Tellingly, within this conceptual scheme he categorizes patriarchal blessings as a patently religious ritual involving individual (rather than group) participation.

5. The full complement of religious expectations from childhood through adulthood—and the corresponding commitment requirements of contemporary Mormonism—are detailed in Hammarberg's forthcoming ethnographic study of the contemporary religious culture of the Latter-day Saints.

6. See Shepherd and Shepherd (1984), Mauss (1994), and Prince and Wright (2005). In a related vein, White (1987, 2008) analyzes the shift in Mormon theology toward "neo-orthodoxy" in the twentieth and twenty-first centuries.

7. Several books have been published on the religious purposes and theological underpinnings of LDS temples by Mormon ecclesiastical authorities—see Packer (1982) and Talmage, Savage, and Heath (1998)—as well as other Mormon authors, including D. Anderson (2010), Bigelow (2009), and Charles (1999), which should be consulted in order to appreciate the transcendent significance that temple worship has assumed for faithful Latter-day Saints.

8. In his forthcoming discussion and analysis of contemporary LDS sealing ceremonies, Hammarberg also points out that LDS temple rituals are polysemic in their classification and may serve a number of interrelated ritual functions. Thus, in addition to analyzing temple rituals as both rites of passage and rites of intensification—two standard ritual categories employed in anthropological studies—Hammarberg also adduces a third ritual category, which he calls "rites of anticipation." This overlaps a good deal with our earlier discussion of compensatory rituals that strengthen peoples' faith in ultimate rewards and shared triumph in compensation for their current sacrificial devotion. Hammarberg's discussion of rites of anticipation is highly relevant for the symbolic understanding of LDS temple rituals in the context of LDS salvation theology and compensatory religious meanings that activate the daily lives of committed church members. On this latter point, see also Davies (2000).

9. In addition to these temples, as of 2009 the LDS Church reported a total of 28,424 congregations (wards and branches) worldwide. See Church of Jesus Christ of Latter-day Saints (2011b).

10. Shepherd and Shepherd (1984, 14).

11. Ibid., 15–17.

12. Our content analysis of LDS general conference addresses from 1830 to 1980 (Shepherd and Shepherd 1984, 73–102) revealed that various "utopian" themes, controversially associated with early Mormonism, virtually vanished in twentieth-century addresses as LDS authorities pursued accommodation to the laws of the land. These were precisely the same themes emphasized so strongly in our sample of early patriarchal blessings—themes subsequently displaced at general conferences of the church by an assortment of nuclear family and respectability themes that were fully compatible with middle-class American values. At the same time, our analysis also demonstrated

the persistent salience of religious authority and ultimate truth claims in the conference addresses of LDS general authorities in both the nineteenth and twentieth centuries.

13. See Weber (1978, 1111–57).

14. Quinn (1997).

15. Prince and Wright (2005).

16. See Shepherd and Shepherd (2009, 743).

17. See Bates and Smith (2003, 1–3) and C. Stephens (1992).

18. The convergence of social movement analysis and organizational theory in the study of maturing movements that institute adaptive normative structures is explored in G. Davis et al. (2005).

19. As of 2009, there were 2,865 LDS stakes organized throughout the world with local jurisdiction over a total of 28,424 wards/branches; see *Deseret News Church Almanac* (2011, 5).

20. Bates (1993); see also Ballif (1992) and Broderick (1995).

21. Bates (1993, 22).

22. In contrast, those Mormons who lose their Latter-day Saint faith and withdraw their commitments, in spite of the manifold group mechanisms available for retaining them in the fold, constitute the primary subject matter for a different book than the one we have written here.

REFERENCES

Ahlstrom, Sydney. 1972. *A Religious History of the American People*. New Haven: Yale University Press.

Alexander, Jeffery C., and Philip Smith, eds. 2005. *The Cambridge Companion to Durkheim*. New York: Cambridge University Press.

Alexander, Thomas G. 1996. *Mormonism in Transition: A History of the Latter-Day Saints, 1890–1930*. Urbana: University of Illinois Press.

Allen, James B. 2002. *No Toil nor Labor Fear: The Story of William Clayton*. Salt Lake City: University of Utah Press.

Allen, James B., Ronald W. Walker, and David J. Whittaker, eds. 2000. *Studies in Mormon History, 1830–1997: An Indexed Bibliography*. With a topical guide to published social science literature on the Mormons, edited by Armand L. Mauss and Dynette Ivie Reynolds. Urbana: University of Illinois Press.

Anderson, Devery. 2010. *Development of LDS Temple Worship, 1846–2000: A Documentary History*. Salt Lake City: Signature Books.

Anderson, Lavina Fielding. 2010. "Dreams of Power: The Patriarchal Blessings of Joseph Smith Sr." Paper presented at the annual meeting of the Mormon Historical Society, Kansas City, Missouri. Copy in authors' possession.

Anderson, Lavina Fielding, and Irene M. Bates. 2001. *Lucy's Book: A Critical Edition of Lucy Mack Smith's Family Memoir*. Salt Lake City: Signature Books.

Arrington, Leonard J. 1986. *Brigham Young: American Moses*. Urbana: University of Illinois Press.

Arrington, Leonard J., and Davis Bitton. 1992. *The Mormon Experience: A History of the Latter-Day Saints*. Urbana: University of Illinois Press.

Arrington, Leonard J., Feramorz Fox, and Dean L. May. 1976. *Building the City of God: Community and Cooperation Among the Mormons*. Salt Lake City: Deseret Book.

Arrington, Leonard J., and Ronald W. Walker. 2004. *Great Basin Kingdom: Economic History of the Latter-Day Saints, 1830–1900*. Urbana: University of Illinois Press.

Backman, Milton V. 1983. *The Heavens Resound: A History of the Latter-Day Saints in Ohio, 1830–1838*. Salt Lake City: Deseret Book.

Balentine, Samuel. 1993. *Prayer in the Hebrew Bible: The Drama of Divine Human Dialogue*. Minneapolis: Augsburg Fortress.

Ballif, Ariel S. 1992. "Patriarch: Stake Patriarch." In *Encyclopedia of Mormonism*, edited by Daniel H. Ludlow, 1064–65. New York: Macmillan.

Bates, Irene M. 1983. "William Smith, 1811–93: Problem Patriarch." *Dialogue: A Journal of Mormon Thought* 16 (2): 11–23.

———. 1993. "Patriarchal Blessings and the Routinization of Charisma." *Dialogue: A Journal of Mormon Thought* 26 (3): 1–29.

Bates, Irene M., and E. Gary Smith. 2003. *Lost Legacy: The Mormon Office of Presiding Patriarch*. Urbana: University of Illinois Press.

Bebbington, David W. 1989. *Evangelicalism in Modern Britain: A History from the 1730s to the 1980s*. London: Routledge.

Beecher, Maureen Ursenbach, and Lavina Fielding Anderson, eds. 1987. *Sisters in Spirit: Mormon Women in Historical Perspective*. Urbana: University of Illinois Press.

Bell, Rob. 2011. *Love Wins: A Book About Heaven, Hell, and the Fate of Every Person Who Ever Lived*. San Francisco: HarperOne.

Bellah, Robert N., Richard Madsen, William M. Sullivan, Ann Swidler, and Steven M. Tipton. 2007. *Habits of the Heart: Individualism and Commitment in American Life*. Los Angeles: University of California Press.

Bennett, Isaiah. 1999. *Inside Mormonism: What Mormons Really Believe*. El Cajon, Calif.: Catholic Answers.

Bennett, Richard E., Susan Easton Black, and Donald Q. Cannon. 2010. *The Nauvoo Legion in Illinois: A History of the Mormon Militia, 1841–1846*. Norman: University of Oklahoma Press / The Arthur H. Clark Company.

Bennion, Janet. 2008. "Mormon Women's Issues in the Twenty-First Century." In *Revisiting Thomas F. O'Dea's "The Mormons": Contemporary Perspectives*, edited by Cardell K. Jacobson, John P. Hoffmann, and Tim B. Heaton. Salt Lake City: University of Utah Press.

Berger, Peter, and Thomas Luckmann. 1967. *The Social Construction of Reality: A Treatise in the Sociology of Knowledge*. New York: Doubleday Anchor.

Bigelow, Christopher K. 2009. *Temples of the Church of Jesus Christ of Latter-Day Saints*. San Diego: Thunder Bay Press.

Bitton, Davis, and Leonard J. Arrington. 1988. *Mormons and Their Historians*. Salt Lake City: University of Utah Press.

Bradley, Martha Sonntag. 1994. "'Seizing Sacred Space': Women's Engagement in Early Mormonism." *Dialogue: A Journal of Mormon Thought* 27 (2): 57–70.

———. 2005. *Pedestals and Podiums: Utah Women, Religious Authority, and Equal Rights*. Salt Lake City: Signature Books.

Bringhurst, Newell G., and Craig Foster. 2008. *The Mormon Quest for the Presidency*. Independence, Mo.: John Whitmer Books.

Bringhurst, Newell G., and John Hamer. 2007. *Scattering of the Saints: Schism Within Mormonism*. Independence, Mo.: John Whitmer Books.

Bringhurst, Newell G., and Darron T. Smith, eds. 2006. *Black and Mormon*. Urbana: University of Illinois Press.

Broderick, Carlfred. 1995. "Uses and Abuses of Patriarchal Blessings in Therapy." Talk given at the annual conference of the Association of Mormon Counselors and Psychiatrists, Salt Lake City. Transcript in authors' possession.

Brodie, Fawn. 1945. *No Man Knows My History: The Life of Joseph Smith*. New York: Alfred A. Knopf.

Bromley, David. 1998. *The Politics of Religious Apostasy: The Role of Apostates in the Transformation of Religious Movements*. Westport, Conn.: Praeger.

———. 2004. "Leaving the Fold: Disaffiliating from Religious Movements." In *The Oxford Handbook of New Religious Movements*, edited by J. R. Lewis, 298–314. New York: Oxford University Press.

Brown, G. Samuel. 2008. "The Translator and the Ghostwriter: Joseph Smith and William Phelps." *Journal of Mormon History* 34:26–62.

Buerger, David John. 2002. *The Mysteries of Godliness: A History of Mormon Temple Worship*. Salt Lake City: Signature Books.

Bush, Lester E., and Armand L. Mauss, eds. 1984. *Neither White nor Black: Mormon Scholars Confront the Race Issue in a Universal Church*. Midvale, Utah: Signature Books.

Bushman, Claudia L., ed. 1997. *Mormon Sisters: Women in Early Utah*. Logan: Utah State University Press.

Bushman, Richard L. 1984. *Joseph Smith and the Beginnings of Mormonism*. Urbana: University of Illinois Press.

———. 1997. "The Visionary World of Joseph Smith." *BYU Studies* 37:183–204.

———. 2005. *Joseph Smith: Rough Stone Rolling*. New York: Alfred A. Knopf.

Charles, John D. [John-Charles Duffy]. 1999. *Endowed from on High: Understanding the Symbols of the Endowment*. Bountiful, Utah: Horizon.

Christie-Murray, David. 1989. *A History of Heresy*. New York: Oxford University Press.

Church of Jesus Christ of Latter-day Saints. 2007. "Membership, Retention on the Rise." *Ensign*, June 2007, 75–80.

———. 2011a. *The Doctrine and Covenants of the Church of Jesus Christ of Latter-day Saints, Containing Revelations Given to Joseph Smith, the Prophet, with Some Additions by his Successors in the Presidency of the Church*. Available at http://www.lds.org/scriptures.

———. 2011b. *Newsroom: The Official Church Resource*. http://www.mormonnewsroom.org/facts-and-stats.

Clayton, William. 2002. "Come, Come Ye Saints." Text by William Clayton (1814–1879) in *Hymns of the Church of Jesus Christ of Latter-day Saints* (2002 ed.). Salt Lake City: Church of Jesus Christ of Latter-day Saints.

Clinton, Catherine, and Christine A. Lunardini. 2006. *The Columbia Guide to American Women in the Nineteenth Century*. New York: Columbia University Press.

Collins, Randall. 2005. *Interaction Ritual Chains*. Princeton: Princeton University Press.

Community of Christ. 2002. *World Conference Bulletin*. Independence, Mo.: Community of Christ.

Compton, Todd. 1997. *In Sacred Loneliness: The Plural Wives of Joseph Smith*. Salt Lake City: Signature Books.

Cooper, Rex E. 1990. *Promises Made to the Fathers: Mormon Covenant Organization*. Salt Lake City: University of Utah Press.

Cornwall, Marie. 1994. "The Institutional Role of Mormon Women." In *Contemporary Mormonism: Social Science Perspectives*, edited by Marie Cornwall, Tim B. Heaton, and Lawrence Alfred Young, 239–64. Urbana: University of Illinois Press.

Cragun, Ryan T., and Ronald Lawson. 2010. "The Secular Transition: Worldwide Growth of Mormons, Jehovah's Witnesses, and Seventh-day Adventists." *Sociology of Religion* 71:349–73.

Cross, Whitney R. 1950. *The Burned-Over District: The Social and Intellectual History of Enthusiastic Religion in Western New York, 1800–1850*. New York: Harper and Row.

Davies, Douglas J. 2000. *The Mormon Culture of Salvation*. Burlington, Vt.: Ashgate.

———. 2002. *Anthropology and Theology*. Oxford: Oxford University Press.

Davis, Derek H., and Barry Hankins, eds. 2003. *New Religious Movements and Religious Liberty in America*. Waco: Baylor University Press.

Davis, Gerald F., Doug McAdam, W. Richard Scott, and Mayor N. Zald. 2005. *Social Movements and Organization Theory*. New York: Cambridge University Press.

Dawson, Lorne L. 1996. "Who Joins New Religious Movements and Why: Twenty Years of Research and What Have We Learned?" *Studies in Religion* 25:193–213.

———. 2008. Comprehending Cults: The Sociology of New Religious Movements. Toronto: Oxford University Press.

Derr, Jill Mulvay, Janath Russell Cannon, and Maureen Ursenbach Beecher. 1992. *Women of Covenant: The Story of Relief Society*. Salt Lake City: Deseret Book.

Deseret News Church Almanac. 2011. Salt Lake City: Church of Jesus Christ of Latter-day Saints.

Doctrine and Covenants. *See* Church of Jesus Christ of Latter-day Saints (2011a)

Dubois, Ellen Carol and Lynn Dumenil. 2005. *Through Women's Eyes: An American History*. New York: Oxford University Press.

Durkheim, Emile. 1968. *The Elementary Forms of Religious Life*. Cambridge: Cambridge University Press.

Edwards, Paul M. 1991. 1985. "William B. Smith: The Persistent 'Pretender.'" *Dialogue: A Journal of Mormon Thought* 18 (2): 128–39.

———. *Our Legacy of Faith: A Brief History of the Reorganized Church of Jesus Christ of Latter Day Saints.* Independence, Mo.: Herald Publishing House.

Ehrman, Bart. 2007a. *Misquoting Jesus: The Story Behind Who Changed the Bible and Why.* San Francisco: HarperOne.

———. 2007b. *The New Testament: A Historical Introduction to the Early Christian Writings.* New York: Oxford University Press.

Eisen, Arnold M. 2000. *Taking Hold of Torah: Jewish Commitment and Community in America.* Bloomington: Indiana University Press.

Erickson, Ephraim E. 1975. *The Psychological and Ethical Aspects of Mormon Group Life.* Salt Lake City: University of Utah Press.

Evans, G. R. 2003. *A Brief History of Heresy.* Blackwell Brief Histories of Religion. New York: John Wiley and Sons.

Flake, Kathleen. 2004. *The Politics of American Religious Identity: The Seating of Senator Reed Smoot, Mormon Apostle.* Chapel Hill: University of North Carolina Press.

Flanders, Robert. 1965. *Nauvoo: Kingdom on the Mississippi.* Urbana: University of Illinois Press.

Fletcher, Holly. 2007. *Gender and the American Temperance Movement of the Nineteenth Century.* New York: Routledge.

Foster, Lawrence. 1979. "From Frontier Activism to Neo-Victorian Domesticity: Mormon Women in the Nineteenth and Twentieth Centuries." *Journal of Mormon History* 6:3–32.

Foucault, Michel. 1995. *Discipline and Punish: The Birth of the Prison.* New York: Vintage Books.

Furniss, Norman F. 1960. *The Mormon Conflict, 1850–1859.* New Haven: Yale University Press.

Geddes, Joseph A. 1922. "The United Order Among the Mormons, Missouri Phase." Ph.D. diss., Columbia University. [Later published as *The United Order Among the Mormons: An Unfinished Experiment in Economic Organization* (Salt Lake City: Deseret News Press, 1924).]

Givens, Terryl L. 1997. *The Viper on the Hearth: Mormons, Myths, and the Construction of Heresy.* New York: Oxford University Press.

———. 2002. *By the Hand of Mormon: The American Scripture that Launched a New World Religion.* New York: Oxford University Press.

Goffman, Erving. 1967. *Interaction Ritual: Essays on Face-to-Face Behavior.* New York: Doubleday Anchor.

Goodbeer, Richard. 1992. *The Devil's Dominion: Magic and Religion in Early New England.* New York: Cambridge University Press.

Gordon, Sarah Barringer. 2001. *The Mormon Question: Polygamy and Constitutional Conflict in Nineteenth-Century America.* Chapel Hill: University of North Carolina Press.

Gottlieb, Robert, and Peter Wiley. 1984. *America's Saints: The Rise of Mormon Power.* New York: G. P. Putnam's Sons.

Grimes, Ronald, ed. 1995. *Readings in Ritual Studies.* Upper Saddle River, N.J.: Prentice Hall.

Hall, David D. 1990. *Worlds of Wonder, Days of Judgment: Popular Religious Beliefs in Early New England.* Cambridge, Mass.: Harvard University Press.

Hammarberg, Melvyn. Forthcoming. *Quest for Glory: The World of the Latter-day Saints.* New York: Oxford University Press.

Hanks, Maxine, ed. 1992. *Women and Authority: Re-emerging Mormon Feminism.* Salt Lake City: Signature Books.

Hansen, Klaus J. 1970. *Quest for Empire: The Political Kingdom of God and the Council of Fifty in Mormon History*. East Lansing: Michigan State University Press.

Hardy, B. Carmon. 2011. "The Persistence of Mormon Plural Marriage." *Dialogue: A Journal of Mormon Thought* 4 (44): 43–105.

Harper, Steven C. 2000. "Infallible Proofs, Both Human and Divine: The Persuasiveness of Mormonism for Early Converts." *Religion and American Culture: A Journal of Interpretation* 10 (1): 99–118.

———. 2008. *Making Sense of the Doctrine and Covenants: A Guided Tour Through Modern Revelations*. Salt Lake City: Deseret Book.

———. 2009. "The Making of Modern Scripture: Latter-day Saints and the Book of Commandments and Revelations." *Mormon Historical Studies* 10 (2): 31–39.

Hartman, Mary S., and Lois W. Banner. 1974. *Clio's Consciousness Raised: New Perspectives on the History of Women*. New York: HarperCollins.

Hartog, Hendrik. 2000. *Man and Wife in America: A History*. Cambridge, Mass.: Harvard University Press.

Henderson, John B. 1998. *The Construction of Orthodoxy and Heresy: Neo-Confucian, Islamic, Jewish, and Early Christian Patterns*. Albany: State University of New York Press.

Hill, Marvin S. 1968. "The Role of Christian Primitivism in the Origin and Development of the Mormon Kingdom, 1830–1844." Ph.D. diss., University of Chicago.

———. 2001. "The First Vision Controversy: A Critique and Reconciliation." *Dialogue: A Journal of Mormon Thought* 15 (2): 31–46.

Howard, Richard P. 1992. *The Church Through the Years*. Independence, Mo.: Herald Publishing House.

———. 2010. *The Ministry of Patriarch-Evangelists: A Brief Historical Survey*. Independence, Mo.: Herald Publishing House.

Howlett, David, John Hamer, and Barbara Walden. 2010. *Illustrated History of the Community of Christ*. Independence, Mo.: Herald Publishing House and John Whitmer Books.

Hughes, Richard T., ed. 1988. *The American Quest for the Primitive Church*. Urbana: University of Illinois Press.

Hughes, Richard T., and C. Leonard Allen. 2000. *Illusions of Innocence: Protestant Primitivism in America, 1630–1875*. Chicago: University of Chicago Press.

Iannaccone, Laurence R., and Carrie A. Miles. 1994. "Dealing with Social Change: The Mormon Church's Response to Change in Women's Roles." In *Contemporary Mormonism: Social Science Perspectives*, edited by Marie Cornwall, Tim B. Heaton, and Lawrence Alfred Young, 265–86. Urbana: University of Illinois Press.

Jacobson, Cardell K., and Lara Burton. 2011. *Modern Polygamy in the United States: Historical, Cultural, and Legal Issues*. New York: Oxford University Press.

Jessee, Dean, Ronald Esplin, and Richard L. Bushman, eds. 2008. *The Joseph Smith Papers: Journals, 1832–1839*. Salt Lake City: Church Historian's Press.

———. 2009. *The Joseph Smith Papers: Revelations and Translation; Manuscript Revelation Books*. Salt Lake City: Church Historian's Press.

Johnson, Sonia. 1981. *From Housewife to Heretic*. New York: Doubleday.

Jungmann, Joseph. 2008. *Christian Prayer Through the Centuries*. Mahwah, N.J.: Paulist Press.

Kanter, Rosabeth Moss. 1972. *Commitment and Community*. Cambridge, Mass.: Harvard University Press.

Kerber, Linda K. 1997. "Republican Mother: Women and Enlightenment—An American Perspective." In *Toward an Intellectual History of Women: Essays by Linda K. Kerber*. Chapel Hill: University of North Carolina Press.

Kertzer, David I. *Ritual, Politics, and Power*. 1989. New Haven: Yale University Press.

Kidd, Thomas S. 2009. *The Great Awakening: The Roots of Evangelical Christianity in Colonial America.* New Haven: Yale University Press.

Kinney, Brandon G. 2011. *The Mormon War: Zion and the Missouri Extermination Order of 1838.* Yardley, Pa.: Westholme Publishing.

Kranish, Michael, and Scott Hellman. 2012. *The Real Romney.* New York: HarperCollins.

Larsen, John. 2008. *Mormonism Refuted in the Light of Scripture and History.* Charleston, S.C.: BiblioBazaar.

Launius, Roger D. 1998. "The Reorganized Church, the Decade of Decision, and the Abilene Paradox." *Dialogue: A Journal of Mormon Thought* 31 (1): 47–65.

Leavitt, Judith W. 1999. *Women and Health in America: Historical Readings.* Madison: University of Wisconsin Press.

Leonard, Glen M. 2002. *Nauvoo: A Place of Peace, a People of Promise.* Salt Lake City: Shadow Mountain Press.

Leonard, Todd J. 2005. *Talking to the Other Side: A History of Modern Spiritualism and Mediumship; A Study of the Religion, Science, Philosophy, and Mediums that Encompass this American-Made Religion.* Lincoln, Neb.: iUniverse.

Lesueur, Stephen C. 1987. *The 1838 Mormon War in Missouri.* Columbus: University of Missouri Press.

Lewis, I. M. 2003. *Ecstatic Religion: A Study of Shamanism and Spirit Possession.* London: Routledge.

Lewis, James R., and Sarah Lewis, eds. 2009. *Sacred Schisms: How Religions Divide.* New York: Cambridge University Press.

Lindgren, Tomas. 2005. "The Narrative Construction of Muslim Prayer Experiences." *International Journal for the Psychology of Religion* 15 (2): 159–74.

Lindsey, William, and Mark Silk. 2005. *Religion and Public Life in the Southern Crossroads: Showdown States.* Walnut Creek, Calif.: AltaMira Press.

Lukes, Steven. 1975. "Political Ritual and Social Integration." *British Journal of Sociology* 9 (2): 289–308.

MacKinnon, William P., ed. 2008. *At Sword's Point: A Documentary History of the Utah War to 1858.* Kingdom in the West: The Mormons and the American Frontier 10. Norman: University of Oklahoma Press / The Arthur H. Clark Company.

Marquardt, H. Michael. 2007. *Early Patriarchal Blessings of the Church of Jesus Christ of Latter-day Saints.* Salt Lake City: The Smith-Pettit Foundation.

Marquardt, H. Michael, and Wesley P. Walters. 1998. *Inventing Mormonism: Tradition and the Historical Record.* Salt Lake City: Signature Books.

Marsden, George M. 2006. *Fundamentalism and American Culture.* New York: Oxford University Press.

Mason, Patrick. 2011. *The Mormon Menace: Violence and Anti-Mormonism in the Postbellum South.* New York: Oxford University Press.

Mathews, Glenna. 1987. *Just a Housewife: The Rise and Fall of Domesticity in America.* New York: Oxford University Press.

Mauss, Armand. 1994. *The Angel and the Beehive: The Mormon Struggle with Assimilation.* Urbana: University of Illinois Press.

———. 2003. *All Abraham's Children: Changing Mormon Conceptions of Race and Lineage.* Urbana: University of Illinois Press.

McGrane, Reginald Charles. 1965. *The Panic of 1837: Some Financial Problems of the Jacksonian Era.* Chicago: University of Chicago Press.

McKinlay, Lynn A. 1992. "Patriarchal Order of the Priesthood." In *Encyclopedia of Mormonism,* edited by Daniel H. Ludlow, 1067. New York: Macmillan.

McLoughlin, William G. 1980. *Revivals, Awakenings, and Reform.* Chicago: University of Chicago Press.

McMurrin, Sterling. 1965. *The Theological Foundations of the Mormon Religion*. Salt Lake City: University of Utah Press.

Merton, Robert K. 1968. *Social Theory and Social Structure*. Glencoe, Ill.: Free Press.

Miles, Carrie A. 2008. "LDS Family Ideals Versus the Equality of Women: Navigating the Changes Since 1957." In *Revisiting Thomas F. O'Dea's "The Mormons": Contemporary Perspectives*, edited by Cardell K. Jacobson, John P. Hoffmann, and Tim B. Heaton. Salt Lake City: University of Utah Press.

Miller, Perry. 1983. *The New England Mind: From Colony to Province*. Cambridge, Mass.: Belknap Press of Harvard University Press.

Moore, R. Laurence. 1986. *Religious Outsiders and the Making of Americans*. New York: Oxford University Press.

Newell, Linda King. 1987. "Gifts of the Spirit: Women's Share." In *Sisters in Spirit: Mormon Women in Historical and Cultural Perspective*, edited by Maureen Ursenbach Beecher and Lavina Fielding Anderson, 111–50. Urbana: University of Illinois Press.

Newell, Linda King, and Valeen Tippetts Avery. 1994. *Mormon Enigma: Emma Hale Smith*. Urbana: University of Illinois Press.

Nibley, Hugh. 1989. *Approaching Zion*. Salt Lake City: Shadow Mountain Press.

Neilson, Reid L., and Terryl L. Givens, eds. 2008. *Joseph Smith, Jr.: Reappraisals After Two Centuries*. New York: Oxford University Press.

Norton, Mary Beth. 1980. *Liberty's Daughters: The Revolutionary Experience of American Women, 1750–1800*. Ithaca: Cornell University Press.

Oaks, Dallin H. 2010. "Fundamental Premises of Our Faith." Talk given to the Harvard Law School. Text available at http://www.mormonnewsroom.org/article/fundamental-premises-of-our-faith-talk-given-by-elder-dallin-h-oaks-at-harvard-law-school.

O'Dea, Thomas F. 1957. *The Mormons*. Chicago: University of Chicago Press.

———. 1961. "Five Dilemmas in the Institutionalization of Religion." *Journal for the Scientific Study of Religion* 1 (1): 30–41.

Ostling, Richard, and Joan K. Ostling. 2000. *Mormon America: The Power and the Promise*. New York: HarperCollins.

Packer, Boyd K. 1982. *The Holy Temple*. Salt Lake City: The Church of Jesus Christ of Latter-day Saints.

Parsons, Elaine Frantz. 2003. *Manhood Lost: Fallen Drunkards and Redeeming Women in the Nineteenth-Century United States*. Baltimore: Johns Hopkins University Press.

Phillips, Rick. 2006. "Rethinking the International Expansion of Mormonism." *Nova Religio: The Journal of Alternative and Emergent Religions* 10 (1): 52–68.

———. 2008. "'De Facto Congregationalism' and Mormon Missionary Outreach: An Ethnographic Case Study." *Journal for the Scientific Study of Religion* 47 (4): 628–43.

Pratt, Parley P. 2000. *Autobiography of Parley P. Pratt, Revised and Enhanced*. Edited by Parley P. Pratt Jr., Scott Facer Proctor, and Maurine Jensen Proctor. Salt Lake City: Deseret Book.

Prince, Gregory A. 1995. *Power from on High: The Development of Mormon Priesthood*. Salt Lake City: Signature Books.

Prince, Gregory A., and W. Robert Wright. 2005. *David O. McKay and the Rise of Modern Mormonism*. Salt Lake City: University of Utah Press.

Quinn, D. Michael. 1980. "The Council of Fifty and Its Members, 1844–1945." *BYU Studies* 20 (2): 1–34.

———. 1992. "Mormon Women Have Had the Priesthood Since 1843." In *Women and Authority: Re-emerging Mormon Feminism*, edited by Maxine Hanks, 365–409. Salt Lake City: Signature Books.

———. 1994. *The Mormon Hierarchy: Origins of Power*. Salt Lake City: Signature Books.

————. 1997. *The Mormon Hierarchy: Extensions of Power*. Salt Lake City: Signature Books.

————. 1998. *Early Mormonism and the Magic World View*. Salt Lake City: Signature Books.

————. 2006. "Joseph Smith's Experience of a Methodist Camp Meeting in 1820." *Dialogue: A Journal of Mormon Thought—Dialogue Paperless: E-Paper #3* (December 20).

————. 2009. "Us-Them Tribalism and Early Mormonism." *John Whitmer Historical Association Journal* 29:94–114.

Roberts, Brigham H. 1965. *A Comprehensive History of the Church of Jesus Christ of Latter-day Saints*. 6 vols. Provo: Brigham Young University Press.

————, ed. 1978. *History of the Church of Jesus Christ of Latter-day Saints*. 7 vols. Salt Lake City: Deseret Book.

Robison, Elwin Clark. 1997. *The First Mormon Temple: Design, Construction, and Historic Context of the Kirtland Temple*. Provo: Brigham Young University Press.

Roof, Wade Clark. 1983. *Community and Commitment: Religious Plausibility in a Liberal Protestant Church*. Cleveland: Pilgrim Press.

Russell, William D. 2003. "The LDS Church and Community of Christ: Clearer Differences, Closer Friends." *Dialogue: A Journal of Mormon Thought* 36 (4): 177–90.

————. 2008. "The Last Smith Presidents and the Transformation of the RLDS Church." *Journal of Mormon History* 35 (3): 46–84.

Rust, Val D. 2004. *Radical Origins: Early Mormon Converts and Their Colonial Ancestors*. Urbana: University of Illinois Press.

Salmon, Marylynn. 1989. *Women and the Law of Property in Early America*. Chapel Hill: University of North Carolina Press.

Sandeen, Ernest. 1978. *The Roots of Fundamentalism: British and American Millenarianism, 1800–1930*. Grand Rapids, Mich.: Baker Book House.

Schneiders, Sandra M. 2001. *Selling All: Commitment, Consecrated Celibacy, and Community in Catholic Religious Life*. Mahwah, N.J.: Paulist Press.

Searle, Howard C. 1992. "Historians, Church." In *Encyclopedia of Mormonism*, edited by Daniel H. Ludlow, 589–92. New York: Macmillan.

Shepherd, Gary. 2007. "Cults: The Social Psychology of." In *The Blackwell Encyclopedia of Sociology*, edited by George Ritzer, 884–87. Oxford: Blackwell.

Shepherd, Gary, and Gordon Shepherd. 1998. *Mormon Passage: A Missionary Chronicle*. Urbana: University of Illinois Press.

Shepherd, Gordon, and Gary Shepherd. 1984. *A Kingdom Transformed: Themes in the Development of Mormonism*. Salt Lake City: University of Utah Press.

————. 1996. "Membership Growth, Church Activity, and Missionary Recruitment." *Dialogue: A Journal of Mormon Thought* 29 (1): 33–57.

————. 2009. "Prophecy Channels and Prophetic Modalities: A Comparison of Revelation in the Family International and the LDS Church." *Journal for the Scientific Study of Religion* 48 (4): 734–55.

Shils, Edward. 1965. "Charisma, Order, and Status." *American Sociological Review* 30 (2): 199–213.

Shipps, Jan. 1985. *Mormonism: The Story of a New Religious Tradition*. Urbana: University of Illinois Press.

————. 1987. Foreword to *Sisters in Spirit: Mormon Women in Historical Perspective*, edited by Maureen Ursenbach Beecher and Lavina Fielding Anderson. Urbana: University of Illinois Press.

————. 1998. "Difference and Otherness: Mormonism and the American Religious Mainstream." In *Minority Faiths and the American Protestant Mainstream*, edited by Jonathan D. Sarna, 81–98. Urbana: University of Illinois Press.

Skinner, Earnest M. 2002. *Joseph Smith, Sr.: First Patriarch to the LDS Church*. Mesa, Ariz.: Palmyra.

Slotkin, Richard. 2000. *Regeneration Through Violence: The Mythology of the American Frontier, 1600–1860*. Norman: University of Oklahoma Press.

Smith, Andrew F. 1997. *The Saintly Scoundrel: The Life and Times of Dr. John Cook Bennett*. Urbana: The University of Illinois Press.

Smith, Joseph Fielding. 1945. *The Restoration of All Things*. Salt Lake City: Deseret Book.

Smith, Lucy Mack. 2007. *History of Joseph Smith by His Mother Lucy Mack Smith: The Unabridged Original Version*. Comp. R. Vernon Ingleton. Foreword by Richard Lloyd Dewey. Provo: Stratford Books.

Sorenson, John L. 2000. "Ritual as Theology and as Communication." *Dialogue: A Journal of Mormon Thought* 33 (2): 117–128.

Spencer, Thomas M., ed. 2010. *The Missouri Mormon Experience*. Columbia: University of Missouri Press.

Staker, Mark L. 2009. *Hearken, O Ye People: The Historical Setting for Joseph Smith's Ohio Revelations*. Salt Lake City: Greg Kofford Books.

Stark, Rodney. 1999. "A Theory of Revelations." *Journal for the Scientific Study of Religion* 38 (2): 287–307.

———. 2005. *The Rise of Mormonism*. Edited by Reid L. Neilson. New York: Columbia University Press.

Stark, Rodney, and William Sims Bainbridge. 1979. "Towards a Theory of Religion: Religious Commitment." *Journal for the Scientific Study of Religion* 18 (2): 117–31.

———. 1985. *The Future of Religion: Secularization, Revival, and Cult Formation*. Berkeley: University of California Press.

Stegner, Wallace. 1992. *The Gathering of Zion: The Story of the Mormon Trail*. Lincoln: University of Nebraska Press.

Stephens, Calvin R. 1992. "Patriarch: Patriarch to the Church." In *Encyclopedia of Mormonism*, edited by Daniel H. Ludlow, 1065–66. New York: Macmillan.

Stephens, Randall J. 2008. *The Fire Spreads: Holiness and Pentecostalism in the American South*. Cambridge, Mass.: Harvard University Press.

Stewart, David G. 2007. *The Law of the Harvest: Practical Principles of Effective Missionary Work*. N.p.: David Stewart.

Talmage, James E., Charles Savage, and Harvard S. Heath. 1998. *The House of the Lord: A Study of Holy Sanctuaries, Ancient and Modern*. Salt Lake City: Signature Books.

Terrin, Aldo Natale. 2007. "Rite/Ritual." In *The Blackwell Encyclopedia of Sociology*, edited by George Ritzer, 3933–36. Oxford: Blackwell.

Tucker, Ruth A. 1989. *Another Gospel: Cults, Alternative Religions, and the New Age Movement*. Grand Rapids, Mich.: Zondervan.

Turner, Frederick Jackson. 1921. *The Frontier in American History*. New York: Henry Holt.

Turner, Victor. 1995. *The Ritual Process: Structure and Anti-Structure*. New Brunswick, N.J.: Aldine Transaction.

Underwood, Grant. 1993. *The Millenarian World of Early Mormonism*. Urbana: University of Illinois Press.

———. 2009. "Revelation, Text, and Revision: Insight from the Book of Commandments and Revelations." *BYU Studies* 48 (3): 68–84.

Van Wagoner, Richard S. 1989. *Mormon Polygamy: A History*. Salt Lake City: Signature Books.

———. 1994. *Sidney Rigdon: A Portrait of Religious Excess*. Salt Lake City: Signature Books.

Vogel, Dan. 1988. *Religious Seekers and the Advent of Mormonism*. Salt Lake City: Signature Books.

————, ed. 1996. *Early Mormon Documents*. Vol. 1. Salt Lake City: Signature Books.

Vogel, Dan, and Brent Lee Metcalfe, eds. 2002. *American Apocrypha: Essays on the Book of Mormon*. Salt Lake City: Signature Books.

Warenski, Marilyn. 1978. *Patriarchs and Politics: The Plight of Mormon Women*. New York: McGraw-Hill.

Weber, Max. 1978. *Economy and Society: An Outline of Interpretive Sociology*. Edited by Guenther Roth and Claus Wittich. Berkeley: University of California Press.

Welch, John W., ed. 2006. *Oliver Cowdery: Scribe, Elder, Witness; Essays from BYU Studies and Farms*. Provo: Neal A. Maxwell Institute for Religious Scholarship.

Welter, Barbara. 1966. "The Cult of True Womanhood, 1820–1860." *American Quarterly* 18 (2): 151–74.

————. 1985. *Dimity Convictions: The American Woman in the Nineteenth Century*. Athens: Ohio University Press.

White, O. Kendall. 1987. *Mormon Neo-orthodoxy: A Crisis Theology*. Salt Lake City: Signature Books.

————. 2008. "Thomas F. O'Dea and Mormon Intellectual Life." In *Revisiting Thomas F. O'Dea's "The Mormons": Contemporary Perspectives*, edited by Cardell K. Jacobson, John P. Hoffmann, and Tim B. Heaton. Salt Lake City: University of Utah Press.

Whittaker, David J. 1987. "The 'Articles of Faith' in Early Mormon Literature and Thought." In *New Views of Mormon History: A Collection of Essays in Honor of Leonard J. Arrington*, edited by Davis Bitton and Maureen Ursenbach Beecher, 63–92. Salt Lake City: University of Utah Press.

Wills, Garry. 2007. *Head and Heart: American Christianities*. New York: Penguin.

Wuthnow, Robert J. 2011. "Talking Talk Seriously: Religious Discourse as Social Practice." *Journal for the Scientific Study of Religion* 50 (1): 1–21.

INDEX

Page numbers in *italics* indicate tables.

Neilson, Reid, 20
new religions. *See* heretical new religions
New York state
    Smith family in, 27–30
    Western part of, 8–9

Oaks, Dallin H., 146 n. 3
Ohio
    Hiram, 33–34
    Kirtland, 31–38, 57–58
oracular prophecy
    description of, 6
    historical containment of, 49–50
    inspirational prophecy compared to, 6–7
    of Smith, 121–22
    ultra-supernaturalism and, 7–9

Packard, Sophia, blessing of, 54
Partridge, Edward, 23
patriarchal blessings. *See also* gender differ-
        ences in patriarchal blessings; sub-
        themes of blessings; themes of
        blessings
    by characteristics of recipients, 93, 93–94
    as commitment mechanisms, 4, 18–19,
        59, 63–65
    communal character of, 57–59
    compensatory ritual character of, 54–57
    contemporary, 107–8, 118–19
    covenantal priesthood lineage and, 60–63
    as extemporaneous, 63, 65, 83
    as father blessing children, 53–54
    first decade of, xi–xii
    as form of prophecy, 18–19, 25
    functions of, 18–19
    as historical documents, 67–69
    institutionalization of, 51
    overview of practice of, xi
    as primary cultic form, 89
    privatization of, 68–69, 108–10, 113–14
    recording of, 66, 67–68
    as ritual, 107–8
    supernatural valence of, 19, 58, 59, 107
    ultra-supernaturalism and, 8, 80
patriarchs. *See also* patriarchal blessings
    authority of office of, 55
    decline of office of, 114–17
    as empowered oracles, 10
    financial remuneration of, 59
    laying on of hands, 55–56
    model for, 51
    origin of office of, 52–54
    primogeniture and, 52
    purpose of office of, 17–18, 52
    Quorum of the Twelve Apostles and, 117

revelations regarding office of, 140–41 n.
    27
role and responsibilities of, 25
sealing authority of, 79
Joseph Smith Sr. as, 25, 53–54, 58–59, 63–
    64, 71
Hyrum Smith as, 52, 71
John Smith as, 46
William Smith as, 52, 71
in stakes, 118
as symbols of God's beneficence, 55–56
performance, rituals as, 54–55
Phelps, William W., 23, 38–39
plural marriage and polygamy. *See also*
        Edmunds-Tucker Bill
    doctrine of eternal exaltation and, 146 n. 3
    in Illinois, 43–44
    "manifesto" ending, 109
    restoration theology and, 62
    RLDS Church and, 13
polarizing character of new religions, 4–6,
    26–27
political economy, integration of church
    into, 15, 108–9
posterity, references to, 79
Pratt, Parley P., 23, 30, 31, 42
preach gospel subtheme of blessings, 95, 97
priesthood. *See also* patriarchs
    of Community of Christ, 149 n. 21
    delegation of authority to, 10
    as eternal and restored, 60–63
    as exclusive to white males, 88–89
    lay, 21
    references to, 95–96, 102
    women in, 13
primitivism, Christian, 21, 23, 31
Prince, Greg, 116
privatization of patriarchal blessings, 68–
    69, 108–10, 113–14
prophecy. *See also* oracular prophecy
    examples of, 121–23
    inspirational, 6–7
    patriarchal blessings as form of, 18–19, 25
    role of in new religions, 20
    true and false, 19–20
prophets. *See also* prophecy
    in contemporary LDS church, 115
    lieutenants of, 106
    words and moral visions of, 5–6
proxy baptisms, 44, 110–11
Puritans of New England, 8

Quincy, Illinois, 41
Quinn, D. Michael, 21, 60, 115–16

Printed in the United States
By Bookmasters